Navigating the Academic Shakeout:

Funding Academia by Building a Grant Culture

Grants Office

IRB
IACUC

Human Resources

Institutional Research

Facilities Services

Campus Security

Accounts Payable

Financial Aid

Campus Housing

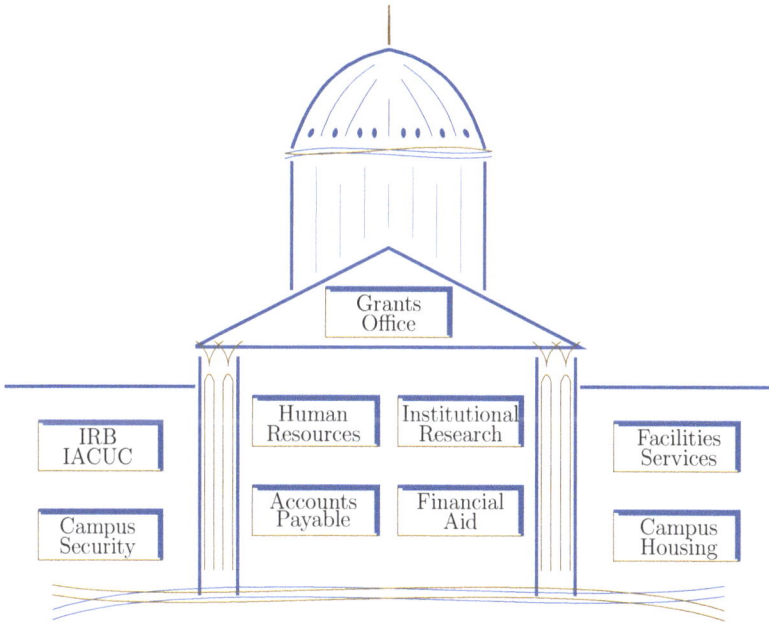

FIORINI & ASSOCIATES

fioriniandassociates.com

PERSEUBLISHING

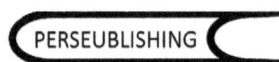

Navigating the Academic Shakeout:
Funding Academia by Building a Grant Culture

by Fiorini and Associates, LLC

Go to fioriniandassociates.com for additional materials.

Published by: Perseublishing, PO Box 181802, Coronado, California 92178, United States of America

Illustrations by Eugene Fiorini

OUR TEAM

We at Fiorini and Associates are knowledgeable about the needs and realities of successful academic grant development and implementation. The authors belong to a consortium of academics (professors, deans, provosts, department chairs), researchers, and industry experts from a variety of disciplines in STEM, social science, and humanities, who are skilled and successful not only at grant "writing," but also well-acquainted with the business processes, research centers, and community organizations that are frequently part of this endeavor.

We do more than promise the "simple step-by-step guide" available in competing volumes; instead we share our detailed knowledge of how the process works, accompanied by real-life examples and practical assignments that will maximize you and your institution's chances of long-term success.

This book represent the collective experience of the authors; however every grant process experience (ideation, planning, writing, administering, reporting, dissemination) is different. We have carefully curated the content in the following chapters to help you acquire the knowledge you need to develop your own best practices.

FIORINI & ASSOCIATES

fioriniandassociates.com

iv

Acknowledgements

The founder, Eugene Fiorini, Ph.D., extends his gratitude to fellow F&A members without whose contributions, guidance, and support this book would not have been possible. F&A appreciates all our friends and colleagues for their encouragement, suggestions, and willingness to review drafts. Special thanks go to Lynette Calvert for her tireless and thorough editing, providing invaluable assistance in rooting out mistakes, clarifying language, and strengthening the overall tone of the book.

Contents

List of Tables

List of Figures

Chapter 1

Today's Higher Ed Landscape

The Current Dilemma

Academic funding has declined, while scholarship requirements and teaching loads have increased. The current higher education landscape requires faculty self-sufficiency. For example:

- An assistant professor must show grant experience as part of his tenure portfolio, but is new to proposals. Where does he begin?
- The science departments learn that austerity moves impact the supply budget and require outside funding for instrumentation. How should they proceed?
- The provost no longer has a faculty development budget, but faculty are still required to maintain professional activities. What strategies might she use to help faculty?

Grants can provide answers, but what is the best path to pursue them?

Chapter 1 Glossary

Throughout this book there will be common terms specific to the grant process, some abbreviated. Explanations will appear in a glossary at the beginning of each chapter, relevant to that chapter's content.

- **Solicitation:** Any type of funding call for proposals from either government, business, or private foundations. There are a variety of names and acronyms, but we will refer to them all as solicitations.

- **Grant culture**: A cornerstone of institutions in which grant development is fully networked, supported, and encouraged, resulting in a sustainable flow of funds to support the entire fundraising effort.

- **Funding agency:** A general term for any organization that offers funding for specific projects.

- **Grantsmanship:** The collection of knowledge, skills, habits and long-term thinking that maximizes successful grant procurement.

- **R1 universities:** High-end research institutions that produce a large number of doctorates and are awarded millions of dollars a year for research.

- **R2 universities:** Institutions with doctoral programs and expectations of research activity, but to a lesser extent than R1 institutions.

1.1 The Academic Shakeout

The United States' greatest global public good is arguably its expansion of universities and research institutes since the mid-twentieth century. These institutions became an international force for advancement in the sciences and arts. Today that foundation is under stress and facing unprecedented challenges, including declining enrollment, soaring tuition, budget pressure, and a disconnect between higher education and employer needs. These trends have created a crisis for many small and mid-size colleges and universities. Some will be forced to merge with other institutions, or face extinction.

According to the National Center for Education Statistics,[1] undergraduate enrollment peaked in 2010 and has been declining ever since. The most visible driver of this crisis is demographics, followed by high tuition costs, student debt, COVID pandemic ripple effects, and growing income inequality. From 2010 through 2023, there has been a 9.9% drop in total college enrollment (undergraduate and graduate). Between 2010 and 2020, undergraduate enrollment declined 12.2%, although graduate enrollment remained steady.[2]

The perceived worth of a college degree has also declined significantly since the 1980s.[3, 4] Recent graduates complain

---

[1] nces.ed.gov/

[2] educationdata.org/college-enrollment-statistics

[3] Harvard Business Review, hbr.org/2021/05/the-u-s-education-system-isn't-giving-students-what-employers-need

[4] shrm.org/resourcesandtools/hr-topics/employee-relations/pages/employers-say-students-aren't-learning-soft-skills-in-college.aspx

that their academic experience is not relevant to the modern workplace. Business leaders, too, lament that graduates are ill-prepared for the corporate world, and cite a lack of "soft skills," such as problem solving, critical thinking, innovation, creativity, teamwork, communication, and the ability to deal with complexity and ambiguity.

Some academics say this mismatch between higher education training and potential employers is due to administrative mismanagement. That disconnect has caused many institutions to lose their way as they push out or dilute liberal arts programs that have taught precisely those "soft skills" for decades.[5]

Coupled with the exogenous pressures mentioned above, these disconnects are likely contributing to more US students choosing to forgo college, and will take considerable effort and communication to close.

In this complex environment, families face a conundrum. A college degree is still about personal growth, fulfillment, and societal participation, but few people can pay for college outright. At this point, families legitimately expect a financial return on their investment. Many question the value of a costly college degree and ask whether it might be better to avoid debt and go directly into the workforce. And yet, a person without a formal degree will inevitably hit the "paper ceiling" that will make it difficult to move ahead. As Doug Shapiro, the executive director of the National Student Clearinghouse Research Center observes: "Without a

---

[5] wsj.com/articles/the-decline-of-liberal-arts-and-humanities-western-philosophy-college-students-major-degrees-progressive-conservative-odysseus-6f327963

dramatic re-engagement in their education, the potential loss to these students' earnings and futures is significant, which will greatly impact the nation as a whole in years to come." [6]

Additionally, as the country grapples with the state of higher education, other nations have expanded educational opportunities. The globalization of higher education erodes an advantage the US once held in two ways. First, other nations are building highly educated, skilled work-forces. As early as 2005, the National Academy of Sciences Council of Competitiveness noted that the growth in the supply pool of science and engineering students overseas put our national competitiveness and national security at risk.[7] Second, for a multitude of reasons, US institutions are no longer always the first choice for a student from a country with an emerging economy.[8] Simply put, as the US loses its qualitative and quantitative edge, American institutions find themselves in competition for overseas students, as well.

Moreover, non-traditional students currently account for a large proportion of the college enrollment population.[9] These students weigh the benefits of an advanced education against the challenges of a shifting economy.

As college and university presidents face the prospect of too few students to fill their classrooms, the strain of these effects creates a sea change in higher education. Many faculty

---

[6] agile-ed.com/higher-education-2022update/

[7] *Rising above the Gathering Storm,* Revisited, National Academies Press, 2005. nap.nationalacademies.org/read/12999/chapter/1

[8] nytimes.com/2018/01/02/us/international-enrollment-drop.html?smid=nytcore-android-share

[9] National Center for Education Statistics

at tuition-dependent colleges and universities know this new reality all too well.

These enrollment trends and the high cost of tuition are not the only pressures on higher education. Others include the economy, the move to remote learning and working, infrastructure issues, societal upheaval, and dwindling federal and state support. This atmosphere creates tremendous need for additional and alternative funding.

These pressures can result in an academic administration's attempts to save money, often at austerity levels, including smaller equipment budgets, decreased support staff, increased teaching loads, more adjunct faculty, consolidation of related institutions, loss of tenure spots, lack of support for the traditional liberal arts, and, particularly, increased requests for tenured faculty to bring in grants (despite the lack of fully staffed grant offices).

In short, the academic world has changed dramatically. This book is in no position to address all these issues in full, but it will help fund needed change at any institution, for administrators as well as for faculty; for example, any grant money the admissions office can use to recruit additional students increases the tuition resource, and saves money on their budget.

As challenging as these circumstances are, effective grantsmanship provides the best opportunity for faculty and administrators to regain control and shape their environment. Through grants, an institution and its faculty can recoup some of what it has lost, including research, equipment, course and program development, student enrichment experiences, outreach to potential students, and professional travel.

1.2 Funding is Available

Grant money exists to ameliorate just about any disconnect or issue. The federal government awards billions of dollars annually via state and local governments; more than 26 federal agencies administer over 1000 grant programs. Additionally, about 140,000 corporations, foundations, trade and professional organizations, religious institutions, and individuals also provide substantial funding. This can include big and small dollar amounts for scholarships, fellowships, seed and pilot grants, research, center grants and other projects. Funding categories can include almost any topic in any discipline.

Faculty at R1 universities know this money exists. These institutions have whole departments devoted to supporting those who develop, submit, and administer grants. They also understand that on average fewer than a quarter of submitted proposals are funded, so instead of giving up, they retool and resubmit rejected grants to different funding agencies one at a time. (Simultaneous submissions to multiple agencies are not allowed.)

Faculty at institutions without these built-in resources need to learn how to locate grant opportunities, write effectively argued proposals, garner support from administrative offices within their own institution, and leverage external collaborative efforts. Briefly, grantsmanship requires the ability to manage expectations; marshal resources; develop fundable ideas; search for solicitations; consider partnerships; develop concepts; budget, write, edit, submit proposals; and administer awarded grants.

This book lays out effective grantsmanship from idea to implementation to future success, and can help fund positive, appropriate institutional change.

Chapter 2

The Basics

Persevere

Grant development can be complex, and often frustrating, with many moving parts. When you encounter problems, or hit roadblocks—and eventually you will—do not despair. There are ways to proceed, even under trying circumstances. This chapter answers questions that commonly arise about the overall process. It also covers strategies, tips, and proactive actions likely to make your proposal more successful. The remaining chapters encourage building a grant proposal draft with "Practice This:" assignments, case studies, checklists, and other materials.

Chapter 2 Glossary

- **Principle Investigator or "PI":** The named senior person in the grant ultimately responsible for administering the program described in a successful proposal.

- **Co-PI:** Additional named senior person who assists the PI in grant administration. Occasionally, there are multiple Co-PIs.

- **Senior Personnel:** Individuals who contribute in a substantive way to the execution of the project. This includes the PI and any Co-PIs.

- **Proposal:** The funding-request documents submitted to an agency in response to a solicitation.

- **Grants Office/Officer:** Generically, the entity responsible for the grant process at an institution: oversight, compliance, dissemination of institutional policies, and proposal review and submission. This may be a designated person, a function of the Development office, a faculty committee, or some other administrative structure.

- **grants.gov:** The website and search engine for all grants offered by the federal government.

- **Reviewer:** A person knowledgeable about the subject who initially evaluates a proposal, usually as part of a panel. The final decision rests with the funding agency. Some agencies compensate reviewers, others do not. Some agencies review in-house, some use external reviewers.

- **Invitation-only:** A type of grant that does not have a published solicitation; the funding agency reaches out to individuals or organizations to request a proposal. Used commonly by large private foundations.

2.1 Who can apply for a grant?

Eligibility for a grant application can depend on a number of requirements, and these differ by funding agency. Most federal and state grants are for US citizens, although green card holders or foreign nationals can contribute to running the program under certain circumstances. Affiliation is critical; grants of any type are almost always given to an organization, rarely to an individual. One exception is fine arts grants which are awarded directly to the artist.

A faculty member or a team at a college or university writes the federal proposal. The college or university submits the funding request to the agency. For some institutions, a provost or dean must sign off on the proposal before submission. Very few federal agencies allow someone to submit a proposal independently. It is the institution that receives the awarded funds. As part of the grant budget, the principal investigator (PI) is paid a stipend to administer the grant, but ownership of the grant itself remains with the institution. The PI is responsible for distributing the funds, with administrative approval. The PI is also responsible for meeting the eligibility requirements, developing the proposal, conducting the work, keeping track of expenditures, and writing the report. This is one reason why closely reading the solicitation is critical.

At the federal level, these rules are fairly uniform; private foundations have their own requirements, which can differ widely, but submission will still depend upon specific procedures. Many of these foundations will state their requisites right up front. If not, ask. The entire range of differences between public and private grant applications is outside the scope of this book, although we will use both in our examples.

2.2 What is the overall process?

A granting organization (private or public) announces its intent to fund a particular type of project by publishing a *solicitation*, a term used here to cover any type of announcement. More specific terms for different types of funding include RFP (Request for Proposal), BAA (Broad Agency Announcements), LRBAA (Long Range Broad Agency Announcements), and RFA (Request for Application), but they are all solicitations.

Eligible organizations write and submit proposals that match the specifics of a solicitation, and then reviewers sort through the proposals and grade them, leading to grant awards for the top applicants.

Sometimes, for example, solicitations have very limited circulation. The Gates Foundation usually asks specific organizations or people to apply for their grants (a process called Invitation-only). Others publish broadly. For instance, the National Science Foundation (NSF) and many other government agencies post solicitations nationally and anyone eligible can apply.

All federal solicitations can be found at the **grants.gov** website. Private ones can be found on foundation websites and in databases. Many of the databases charge fees, but even the expensive ones usually have a free trial or restricted access account. (See *Chapter 3* for details and *Chapter 4* for search examples.)

2.3 Are most proposals funded?

Unfortunately the short answer is NO. Depending on the granting organization, fewer than a quarter of submitted proposals are successful overall. Among the obstacles to a successful proposal are money limitations at the funding agency, politics, inexperienced grant reviewers, multiple similar submitted proposals, economics, concerns at the funding agency about the applicant institution's ability to complete the program, insufficiently innovative ideas, and/or lack of adherence to the specifics of the solicitation.

Whether the first proposal is successful or not, keep trying: success rates improve after a few tries. Even the most skilled grant developers lose out sometimes due to things beyond their control. For example, if a solicitation receives a large number of responses, there may not be enough funding to cover every good proposal. Sometimes there are unknown agendas driving the reviewers.

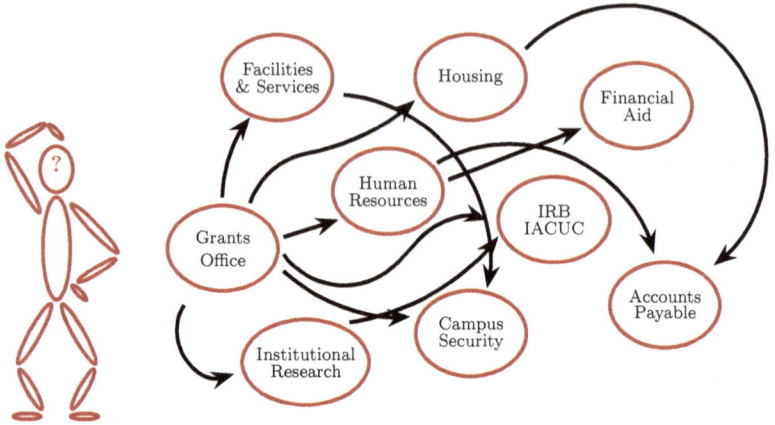

Figure 2.1: Campus departments

2.4   What improves funding success?

Despite some unavoidable uncertainty in the grant development process, there are controllable elements:

- **Get to know your institution both horizontally (colleagues) and vertically (administration and staff).** This will uncover hidden resources, help develop partnerships, and contribute to a culture of grant development, which will benefit all of the stakeholders on campus.

- **Allow ideas to evolve.** In addition to meeting solicitation requirements, initial grant ideas often need to adapt to prevailing circumstances. Document that evolution, both to give credit where due and to capture additional grant ideas spawned by vigorous discussion.

- **Contact college associations and professional organizations for assistance.** These groups, often underutilized, may have accessible resources such as grant databases, alerts, networking opportunities, and even funding of their own. Additionally, they can serve as partners or schedule introductions to potential partners in their system.

- **Learn about current themes in funding.** Right now, for example, there is an emphasis on workforce development. Another popular theme, particularly after the pandemic, is public health and health equity. Knowledge of the political climate can help position a grant request, so keep up to date; it changes over time.

- **Start by going after smaller grants first.** Look for solicitations that support conferences or workshops rather than major programs. This helps build a track record that will impress reviewers on larger grants. Use that same track record to lobby your upper administration for more support.

- **Plan pro-actively.** It is just as important as writing. For example, start thinking early about the logistics of the grant. Communicate with every needed campus department, particularly the grants or development office, but also security, housing, grounds, dining, and so on. Start making a list of budget items and costs. Establish procedures for collecting data. (See *Chapter 9* for details.)

- **Read the funding request thoroughly.** It is critical to follow exactly all the guidelines and rules in the solicitation. This includes minutiae as well as content: number of pages, margins, fonts, citation format, literature search, and so on. For example, a single reference not cited in the text might reduce the grade from a reviewer.

- **Ask for help from a funding agency representative.** After studying the fine print in an interesting solicitation, try to make contact with someone at the agency to answer any questions. While program directors will not influence the reviewers, they can provide context, history, and helpful tips. These informal conversations can get a proposal closer to the finish line. Also, always check that a solicitation is legitimate. Beware of scams promising "free money from the government" on the internet and various media outlets. If in doubt, contact the funding agency.

- **Serve as a reviewer for a funding agency.** Not all agencies have external reviewers. If possible, reviewing is an excellent way to learn the internal process. Most federal agencies have review panels; contact the program manager (name available on the agency website).

- **When resubmitting, continue allowing ideas to evolve.** A different lens on a problem or submitting to another solicitation may be more successful at obtaining a grant, while at the same time preserving the foundational idea and any boilerplate language (facilities statement, for example).

- **Keep trying.** No one is successful on every proposal; experience will help better your average.

2.5   Getting Started

Often, the scarcest resource is time, but flexibility, mentoring, and institutional support are also critical to grant development success. Expect that you will have to change the way you do business. This may include accepting mentoring from more experienced colleagues, acknowledging new ways of thinking, and expanding your circle of acquaintances.

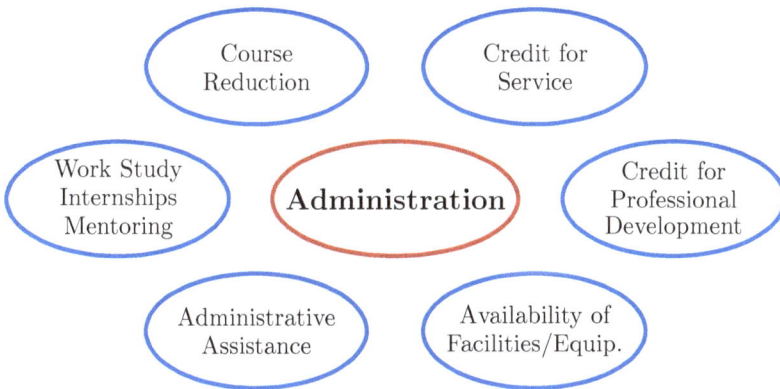

Figure 2.2: Administrative support

First, it is essential to secure administrative support to help alleviate time and resource pressures that can impede a successful grant process. Faculty responsibilities of teaching, service, and scholarship often leave no room for grant pursuit. *Figure 2.2* summarizes some types of administrative support. Negotiation for this support should begin early, and will likely be ongoing as a grant culture develops. Course or service reduction will allow more time to manage grant projects. Access to facilities and equipment for grant activities will streamline the logistics. Additional assistance from staff, work study students, and mentors will distribute the workload. Professional development credit and travel funds also provide incentives for faculty to pursue grants.

Other strategies to consider appear below.

- **One helpful structure is teamwork.** Done well, it substantially reduces the workload on each participating person. Additionally, teams generally come up with more nuanced, complex, and interesting ideas that fare well in a proposal. Consider interdisciplinary groups for more broad-based or outreach projects.

- **Partner with other universities, colleges, or college consortia.** For a smaller college, partnership helps to make the institution look more visible and impressive. It also increases the availability of facilities, resources, expertise among senior personnel, and access to a broader scope of grants. (Details on this in *Chapter 5.*)

- **Network.** A 2014 article from *Non-Profit Quarterly* is still relevant and worth a full read.[1] Many of the largest private funding agencies have an invitation-only policy for grant proposals. Most will not even read an initial letter of inquiry from anyone else. This can look like an impenetrable obstacle, but the key

---

[1]Scaling the Wall: 5 Ways to Get Unsolicited Proposals Heard—nonprofit quarterly.org/scaling-the-wall-getting-your-grant-proposal-heard

is finding ways to get on their radar. The article's suggested strategy is to meet and exchange information with organization representatives at conferences and other venues, and then send helpful followup information after researching their websites for needs, focus, and gaps. *Do not pitch a proposal unless asked.* This is important. An invited grant proposal becomes more likely once your name recognition increases, but a hurried sales pitch will tend to do the opposite.

PRACTICE THIS: Find current resources.

The first step in an apparently overwhelming process is to find out what grant resources and support you can access right now at your own institution. Investigate and list potentially helpful people, committees, benefits, and offices, as well as any academic consortium memberships:

- Does the administration value grant development?
- Do they offer release time for it?
- Is grant development considered a plus in a tenure package? As a positive for promotion?
- Talk to the office or faculty committee charged with obtaining grants. How can they help?
- Seek out colleagues who write grants. What paths do they take? Are they willing to act as mentors?
- Are administrative assistants available to help for some parts of a project?
- Are commercial databases of grants available for searching?

Chapter 3

Ideation and Solicitation

CASE STUDY: Idea Evolution

The spotted lanternfly (*Lycorma delicatula*) threatened many agricultural crops and hardwood trees.[a] The timing of the infestation coincided with Professor Flowers' search for a new way to encourage minority high school students to consider STEM as a career. A small grant funded the initial summer workshop, in which a team of scientists and undergraduates guided high-schoolers as they investigated the problem and conducted experiments on the behavior and life cycle of the spotted lanternfly. Subsequent grants secured a total of $60,000 for the program over a three-year period.

[a]US Department of Agriculture Animal and Plant Health Inspection Service—aphis.usda.gov/aphis/home/.

Chapter 3 Glossary

- **Ideation:** The process of formulating, discovering, discussing, and conceptualizing project ideas and then matching one or more of them to appropriate funding solicitations.

- **Commercial grant databases:** These specialized search engines, comprehensive although often expensive, provide access to thousands of solicitations at hundreds of granting agencies. (See *Section 3.4* for some examples.)

- **Merit criteria:** This describes Intellectual Merit, Broader Impact, and Broadening Participation, three types of statements that are useful in enriching any proposal with context. (See *Section 3.2* for definitions and examples.)

- **tax form 990:** A public document that non-profits must submit to the IRS. As grant seekers prepare their proposals, they can get useful information on funding agencies' financial health and fitness for a project from these disclosures.[1] The IRS[2], and some of the larger grant search engines maintain lists of these forms.

- **Investigator-initiated research:** Used mostly by the National Institutes of Health (NIH), it allows research scientists in medical fields to suggest projects without a specific solicitation.

---

[1] instrumentl.com/blog/how-to-read-form-990s-to-find-funders

[2] Tax Exempt Organization Search (TEOS): irs.gov/charities-non-profits/tax-exempt-organization-search

3.1 Devise Project Ideas

Which comes first—idea or solicitation? Some academics have plenty of ideas for grants, so they need to search for just the right solicitation. Others find an interesting solicitation and then do some thinking about a project that might match it well. Still others review several resources and ideas for a proposal before settling on a solicitation/idea combination. All of these approaches can work well.

Inspiration is everywhere. Sub-fields of established fields merge to create new fields (computational biology, for example) that are rich sources of new inquiry. Even initially unpromising ideas might be fruitfully reconfigured into a grant by adding multiple ideas or disciplines together. Whether reading, having a conversation, consuming news, or just observing, see if you can connect the dots to a grant or an activity.

The idea generation process need not take much extra time; pull "new research" out of what you already do—curriculum reviews, new/updated courses, student assignments, service learning work, new teaching ideas, world/national news. The key is developing instincts to recognize when a fledgling grant idea appears, documenting it, and turning it into a fundable question. (See *Chapter 6* on Concept Papers as a documentation tool.) Allow a creative environment to exist for you to explore and imagine. Successful grant development is usually not a solo process, either. (See the "speed dating" suggestion in *Section 5.3* for finding collaboration partners.)

Grants can help support the entire institution indirectly by increasing the number of majors in your department, drawing new undergraduates to the school, encouraging existing ones to get involved, and providing funds for new faculty. In the lanternfly project example, the high school students said afterward that they were now interested in attending the sponsoring college. One young man, who had been told incorrectly that he was not good at math, chose to double up on advanced math courses to help prepare for a potential career in biochemistry. Several students who had not considered college were now focused on it and knew they were capable of success.

3.1.1   Brainstorming Examples

Look around. Maybe you have been focused mostly on teaching, or just got started doing research, or now need to fill a funding cut or support your own salary. Ask yourself these questions:

- Do you have an idea that might be suitable for a grant? Are there professional activities that would advance your career? How will a project developed through that lens further both your goals and the institution's mission?

- Is there a gap in an area of your discipline that could be filled after investigation? Identify an emerging topic within your field (or at the intersection of two or more fields) that would benefit from concentrated attention.

- Would additional equipment or services enhance your scholarly efforts? Are there teaching resources (either equipment, supplies, or curriculum improvements) that would improve your classroom environment?

- Might you want to develop workshops or conduct community outreach to potential students or non-profits? Look around your community for a social justice issue (water quality, housing, policing, etc), and use this topic to develop a conference or workshop. Consider sustainability, for example, and not only with a STEM focus. Arts & Humanities and the social sciences play a central role in sustainability as well.

- Current issues can be a rich source of ideas: Emerging diseases, health equity, digital transformation, invasive species, distribution systems, historical context for recent events, artificial intelligence, and online misinformation, to name only a few. New issues can be vague, but that leaves lots of room for inquiry.

- If you need to do off-site research, travel grants are available from multiple granting organizations for a variety of purposes (a worked out example appears in *Section 4.2*).

- Some ideas that might inspire good projects appear in *Appendix A*.

Funding agencies are often interested in what is current and captures the public's attention. As you build proposal development into your group's long-term planning, it is important to understand that federal agencies rely on the grant-seeking community itself as they determine evolving needs and priorities. The solicitation process is a system of interplay between the funding agency and prospective grantee.

At public discussions and conferences, the first question from the audience is usually: "What projects are you looking to fund?" Quite often, the response from agency representatives is clear: "That's what you should be telling us." Being aware of changes and developing trends that point the way to new field creation can lead to many grant opportunities.

Moreover, cooperation among organizations can strengthen the overall appeal of a proposal by increasing available facilities and resources, expanding the scope of the research, and broadening the impact of the project. (See *Chapter 5* on Partnerships.)

While brainstorming, remember to define your goals for the project. What are some of the hurdles you will need to overcome to implement it? Who might you work with? Can you involve undergraduates?

While many of your ideas will be expandable, it may be best to start off with a straightforward or introductory grant proposal—for example, hosting a conference. How would you convince the funding agency of the importance and uniqueness of the conference topic? What are some of the logistics to consider when organizing such a professional gathering?

3.2   Three Crucial Merit Criteria

Intellectual merit, broader impact, and broadening participation statements can make the difference between whether a proposal is accepted or denied. They explain how the project will benefit a wider audience, something central to many funding agency missions. Spend some time on this. Some solicitations require statements in one or more of these areas. Even if yours does not, touching on how your proposal advances one or more of these criteria will improve its chances of success.

The examples below are from a proposal to improve science learning for students in low-income families, through partnership with a family service organization (FSO).

3.2.1 Intellectual Merit

Intellectual merit is a statement about the original contributions that the research will make to knowledge in an area of study. How will the project advance what we collectively know?

Example: "*The project* leverages a flexible intellectual process that maximizes the agency of young people in their communities by engaging them in problem-solving relevant to their environments. It advances understanding of science capital effectiveness in practical scenarios and thus has the potential to be transformative for supplemental learning practices. As participants progress, the inquiry-based, differentiated learning environment will adapt to needs and innovations that arise. FSOs advance STEM learning and thus enrich the intellectual focus of science capital on student agency and science identity. Ultimately, this project seeks to better understand the potential of a model for implementing place-based units within a sustainable STEM learning ecosystem."

3.2.2   Broader Impact

Broader Impact encompasses the project's potential to benefit society and contribute to specific, desired societal outcomes.

Example: "By promoting STEM concepts as tools for inquiry into community issues, *the project* has potential transformative benefits to society at three levels: individual, family, and community.   Individual students will be empowered to use STEM tools to better understand the world around them, feel more confident in STEM discussions with a broader audience, and be more likely to choose a career based in science or mathematics.   With more classroom-ready materials and support at their disposal, *the project* will establish a cohort of FSO instructors better able to use and promote inquiry-based, differentiated learning.   They will also see the value for themselves in drawing more people into the process.   Focusing on community issues invites connections between the humanities, social sciences, and STEM.   *The project* will assist the entire family to constructively interact with schools, teachers, and administrators. Parents and guardians will be better positioned to understand administrative decisions, challenge course placement if needed, and take advantage of college-readiness information.   Dissemination of the program materials and research findings to multiple communities beyond the original program will enrich the STEM learning ecosystem across multiple academic levels and educational formats, encouraging FSOs to play a more active partnership role with cooperating schools."

3.2.3 Broadening Participation

Broadening Participation answers the question, "How does this work contribute specifically to building a diverse and capable workforce vital to maintaining the nation's standard of excellence?"

Example: "STEM degree production is not keeping pace with the demand for STEM talent...and must move beyond simple degree completion rates to more sophisticated measures." [3] *The project* broadens participation of underrepresented groups by piloting a robust STEM learning experience for this cohort that is sustainable, widely applicable to many communities, delivered by trusted community members, and disseminated well beyond the immediate environment. Students will contribute enthusiasm and develop agency while investigating STEM to solve current community/social issues.

The *pipeline* model of success, e.g., completion of higher education degrees, is less available to underrepresented students. The *agency* model opens more doors to that pipeline. It encourages more students because it recognizes the many ways that STEM is relevant, not only in career choices, but also in everyday life. It focuses on valuing people and their culture as they participate in creating a STEM ecosystem that increases access to science capital components, and thus develops science identity and agency for students and families as it applies STEM problem-solving tools to current community/social issues. *The project* supports and relies

---

[3] American Institutes for Research, (2012) "Broadening Participation in STEM: A Call to Action," NSF HRD-1059774.

on an underutilized resource, FSOs, to deliver the program, serve as the instruments to sustain it beyond the pilot, and widen the economic reach of first-generation citizens. FSOs are well placed to ensure that increasing numbers of students have varied, meaningful, and in-depth access to STEM, and because of the trust FSOs have built, they can encourage families to be engaged and supportive. Because not all students respond well in a classroom setting, *the project* places them in an environment where those students are more comfortable learning: their own communities."

3.3   Is the project grant-fundable?

This is important. Some ideas simply will not win grants and others can be revised so that they will.

- If a program already has ongoing funding, getting more money for exactly the same program would be a tough sell.

  Possible Solution: identify a new need or direction that is not covered by the current funding, and resubmit with that as the focus.

- If the research is not championed in some way by the institution, the funder may decline the proposal.

  Possible Solution: show your administration how grant money in one area will benefit the entire institution, not just a small part of it.

- If research requires an expensive piece of instrumentation, but access to the same instrument at another university is available, the request may be denied.

Possible Solution: resubmit with reasons why current access is insufficient, and/or how more researchers will benefit by a second instrument in the region.

- If the scope of the idea is too large, or unfocused, or the reviewers doubt a small school can handle it, they may say no.

  Possible Solution: an external partner could be beneficial in several ways: supplement available resources, expand available expertise, more clearly focus the project scope, etc.

Sometimes none of the above will be feasible, in which case contact the development office for other types of funding (donations, etc.).

3.4 Databases of Solicitations

Commercial grant databases can be seriously expensive; ask your grants office, college library, professional organizations, or academic consortium to see if they subscribe to any of them. Fortunately, some lower cost commercial databases exist that might be worth a look, and some of the higher cost ones have free searching or browsing for useful, if limited, information.[4]

There are dozens of funding search engines (database collections) and online lists that pull together a large number of solicitations in many areas. In addition to grants, some list

---

[4]This information is current as of the publication of this book.

scholarships, fellowships, visiting appointments, and other opportunities. The following are examples—others exist.

- The main federal search engine is grants.gov, free and comprehensive for all federal grants in any discipline or agency. (See *Section 4.1.2* for a fully worked out example.)

  The National Endowment for the Arts maintains a page of federal grants for Research on the Arts and Human Development as well.

  arts.gov/initiatives/arts-human-development-task-force/ additional-resources/federal-funding-resources-research-arts-human-development

- A yearly membership to the *Chronicle of Philanthropy* magazine, (about $100/year) offers, in addition to their fundraising news and profile articles, free full access to the Grant Station search engine, which covers international as well as US grants. Grant Station also sports an unusual search interface, with lots of help. (See *Section 4.2* for an example using this search engine.) Training webinars and courses are available there at additional cost.

  Through the Chronicle: philanthropy.com/grants

- The Foundation Directory Online (FDO)[5] is expensive. If your college does not have a subscription, FDO also has a free "Quick Start" account that provides ba-

---

[5]FDO is accessed through the CANDID portal and is comprehensive for foundations. Guidestar is a section of CANDID that can provide additional useful information. guidestar.org/

sic contact information for thousands of foundations.

fconline.foundationcenter.org/welcome/quick-start

- InstrumentL is another large, expensive database similar to the Foundation Directory. A portion of it offers significant free browsing and quick find features. Additionally, there is a comprehensive posting about how to read the important non-profit tax form 990 to extract grant information and evaluate a funding agency's "fit" for your project.

instrumentl.com/blog/how-to-read-form-990s-to-find-funders
instrumentl.com

- The Grant Forward search engine focuses entirely on STEM funding resources for academic researchers. It is only available to institutional subscribers, not to individuals. It is worth asking your institution to subscribe if you are a STEM faculty member.

grantforward.com/index

- William & Mary College maintains substantial free lists of both humanities and science funding resources. Many other institutions do the same.

wm.edu/offices/sponsoredprograms/funding/humanities
wm.edu/offices/sponsoredprograms/funding/sciences

- The Council on Foundations has a free Community Foundation Locator.

cof.org/page/community-foundation-locator

- ScientifyResearch.org is a Europe-based grant search

engine, in English, that databases grants around the world. They have a free membership as well as three levels of paid membership.

scientifyresearch.org

- One low cost database that covers a lot of large and small private and regional grants is Grants for US. It is not affiliated with the US government.

fundsforngos.org/about-us.

Subscribe to alerts and browse their offerings for free; paid members can search for about $10/month.

grantsforus.io

- Grant Gopher concentrates on non-profit, school, and municipality grants. They have a free "Lite" account that allows searching, but only gives the top five hits for each search, and a Pro account that costs about $100/year. They also have sample proposals.

grantgopher.com

3.4.1   Grant Training

- For in-depth federal grant training, the Grants Learning Center is the place to begin; they have an extensive set of free training modules. Go to grants.gov and click "Learn" in the menu bar to get started.

- For additional training, the commercial Grant Training Center is available for a fee.

granttrainingcenter.com

3.4.2 Investigator-Initiated Opportunities

A smaller subset of grants, referred to as "investigator-initiated," (mostly health-related) are awarded without a specific solicitation. A major funding agency of such grants is the National Institutes of Health (NIH) and its subdivisions, but other agencies have some as well. Additional grants of this type are available through insurance and pharmaceutical companies, and professional organizations such as the American Heart Association. These always require advanced credentials and experience, and are most frequently awarded for clinical studies, although some cover things like undergraduate training.

3.5 More Funding Sources

The various dedicated grant search engines and lists highlighted here are not the only places to look for funding. Sometimes even a Google search will pull up useful hits (although admittedly you will have to sift through quite a few pages to find promising ones). For some requests, an institutional benefactor or other donor might be a better option than a grant. Consult with your development office in these cases. Even if you do not find an opportunity, you may discover sources that would lead to good external partnerships, or get some new ideas.

3.5.1 State and City Funding Agencies

Most states have Humanities and/or Arts Councils, as do some cities and counties (a few municipal funding agencies appear in *Table 3.1.*) Many supply sponsorships across all of the arts to support local artistic projects). There are many others.

Two examples of the kind of projects supported by a municipal governments are funding artists to create murals on city buildings or funding the restoration or investigation of local historical sites. One specific example is offered by the Los Angeles County Arts and Culture Council (LACAC). It has a two-year funding opportunity for arts organizations that positively impact the community.

Table 3.1: A Sample of state and municipal funding agencies

Agency	URL
Georgia Humanities Council	georgiahumanities.org
Humanities Texas	humanitiestexas.org/home
Idaho Humanities Council	idahohumanities.org
California Arts Council	arts.ca.gov
NY Foundation for the Arts	nyfa.org
LA County Arts and Culture[6]	lacountyarts.org

3.5.2   Other Organizations with Grant Opportunities

Professional organizations often offer grants of various kinds, some nationally or regionally, some confined to a single city. *Table 3.2* is a partial list. There are many others.

---

[6]LACAC supports 2-year grants for arts organizations that impact community.

Table 3.2: Sample of organizations that offer grants.

Organizations
Modern Language Association
This site (including Northeast Modern Language Association) provides a platform for members to share scholarly and teaching experiences and discuss current trends.
mla.org/Resources/Career/MLA-Grants-and-Awards
Mathematical Association of America
MAA provides several small grants (\$6,000 to \$30,000) to support K-16 mathematics-related projects.
ams.org/opportunities
American Chemical Society
This international society offers funding to advance the chemical sciences through research, education, and community projects.
acs.org/funding.html?selectedPage=1
American Heart Association
This organization provides awards in line with their mission.
professional.heart.org/en/research-programs/aha-funding-opportunities
American Philosophy Association
This organization supports projects and initiatives beneficial to the philosophical community. The awards are generous, but restricted to research only.
amphilsoc.org/grants/research

Continued on next page

Table 3.2 – continued from previous page

Organizations

Princeton University Library
This site maintains a good list of professional organizations in the social sciences.
libguides.princeton.edu/gradprofessionalorgs/social-sciences

The Open Education Database (OEDb)
The OEDb blog posted a lengthy list of funding agencies, mostly but not exclusively professional organizations.
oedb.org/ilibrarian/100_places_to_find_funding_your_research

College Arts Association
This group is the world's largest professional association for artists, art historians, designers, and other art professionals. Search "grants" to get a list of arts and design grants.
collegeart.org/search/index

US Commission of Fine Arts
This group funds mostly non-profits in Washington DC.
cfa.org

3.5.3   Private Funding Organizations

There are other funding organizations beyond what is given in *Sections 3.5.1 and 3.5.2*. Some of these are large, some small, some niche, some expansive, some personal, and some family-driven. *Table 3.3* lists just a few examples of these; there are many more.

Table 3.3: A sample of other funding organizations.

Funding Organization
Robert Wood Johnson Foundation
This organization funds a wide swath of health and health equity projects.
rwjf.org/en/grants/active-funding-opportunities.html?o=1&us=1
Russel Sage Foundation
This group funds social science research on pressing social & economic topics.
russellsage.org
Horowitz Foundation
This group funds social policy projects.
horowitz-foundation.org/grant-info
JM Kaplan Fund
This group funds mostly invitation-only grants across a wide range of social justice, conservation, art, and environment areas.
jmkfund.org/
Tinker Foundation
This foundation specializes in economic and social development in Latin America. They accept letters of inquiry; grant proposals are invitation-only.
tinker.org/institutional-grants-apply-page
Bill & Melinda Gates Foundation
This foundation funds mostly invitation-only projects, although there are a few open solicitations.
gatesfoundation.org

PRACTICE THIS: Defining Intellectual Merit

In many ways, a grant proposal is similar to a dissertation research plan. It needs to convince a committee to move ahead with the work, usually with one of two rationales (both of which contribute to intellectual merit):

- The project will break new ground by developing a new theory, application, device, or methodology. As a result, the effort will impact state-of-the-art research or deliver to the public and private sector societal benefits.

OR

- The project will investigate existing data and unearth findings that will challenge or overturn conventional thought. Outcomes might impact policy development, update core curricula, or create special focus areas and certificate programs.

Write an intellectual merit statement on one or more of your ideas. It is important that your proposal be compelling. Your narrative provides an opportunity to demonstrate how your project is exceptional. Focus on making your strongest case with the intellectual merit component, assisted by broader impact and broadening participation statements.

Chapter 4

Solicitation Search Process

The Search Begins

This chapter will provide search examples that cover multiple disciplines using different grant search engines and strategies. We start with federal grants, helpfully located at a single website: grants.gov. Although STEM grants often get the most press, there are federal grants for humanities or social science projects as well. No matter your discipline or department, we recommend first focusing on federal offerings because the structure and expectations required by federal agencies can be transferable to other funding agencies.

Chapter 4 Glossary

- **Catalog of Federal Domestic Assistance** (CFDA): Currently undergoing substantial change, but still useful in federal solicitation searches, the CFDA number is a general classification assigned to most federal grants and cooperative agreements. The description page of every federal solicitation lists its CFDA.

- **Opportunity Number:** Similar to the CFDA, but more specific. Each solicitation of any kind has its own unique opportunity number.

- **Posted and Forecasted:** These are two useful basic descriptors found in grants.gov. "Posted" refers to currently active solicitations. "Forecasted" refers to potent future solicitations.

- **Unrestricted:** This category in grants.gov indicates any type of entity listed is eligible to apply for the solicitation.

- **Federal Agency Abbreviations:** All agencies that publish solicitations are identified on search engines by a three-letter abbreviation. (See *Table 4.1* for ones commonly referenced.) The University of California San Diego library maintains a comprehensive list of government acronyms and abbreviations.[1]

---

[1] GovSpeak (ucsd.libguides.com/govspeak): a Guide to Government Acronyms and Abbreviations.

Table 4.1: Federal agency abbreviations

Abbrev.	Agency
NSF	National Science Foundation
NIH	National Institutes of Health
NEH	National Endowment for the Humanities
NEA	National Endowment for the Arts
DOE	Department of Energy
HHS	Health and Human Services
HUD	Housing and Urban Development
DHS	Department of Homeland Security
DOD	Department of Defense
DOT	Department of Transportation
DOC	Department of Commerce

4.1 Finding Federal Solicitations

All federal solicitations appear on grants.gov. Almost all searches there follow the process outlined in *Table 4.2* and diagrammed in *Figure 4.1*.

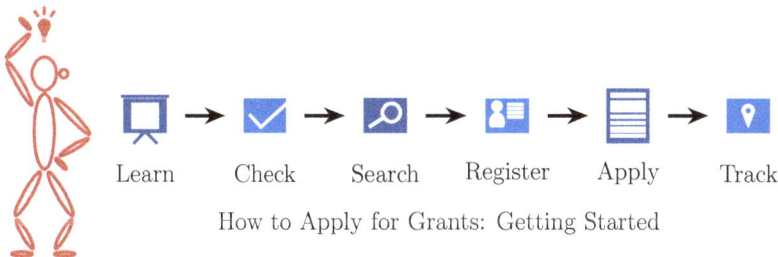

Learn   Check   Search   Register   Apply   Track

How to Apply for Grants: Getting Started

Figure 4.1: Federal grant application process

Table 4.2: The grants.gov federal grant application process

Section	Process
Learn	First, learn as much as possible about the federal grant application process: active solicitations, terminology, systems, programs, etc. The *Learn Grants* tab at grants.gov contains this information and more.[2]
Check	Next, check who is eligible to apply for federal grants. The *Grant Eligibility* subtab under the *Learn Grants* tab is where to find this information.
Search	The *Search Grants* tab is where to begin looking for active solicitations. (See *Figure 4.2*.)
Register	In order to submit a proposal through grants.gov, the next step is to create an account. Both individuals and organizations can register. Click the *Register* button to access the registration page.
Apply	"Workspace" is the standard platform by which organizations or eligible individuals apply for federal grants on grants.gov. To create your Workspace, click the *Applicants* tab, then scroll down to "Workspace Overview."
Track	Once a proposal has been submitted, its status can be checked using the grants.gov tracking number.

---

[2] grants.gov/learn-grants/grants-101/

4.1.1 Getting to Know grants.gov

On grants.gov click the *Search Grants* tab, which opens an elaborate screen with a large number of search features: keywords, opportunity number, CFDA, and then a few selectable options including opportunity status, funding instrument type, eligibility, category of interest, and federal agency. Click an arrow to the left of any option to drop the selection list. (See *Figure 4.2.*)

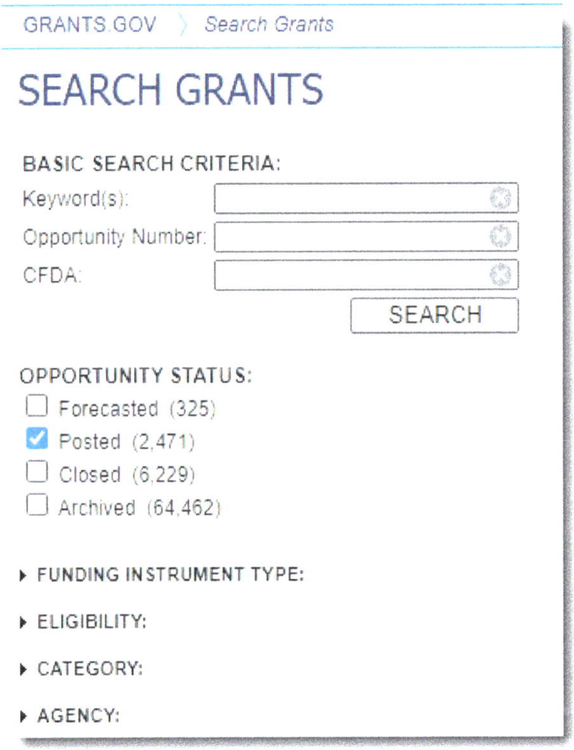

GRANTS.GOV ⟩ *Search Grants*

SEARCH GRANTS

BASIC SEARCH CRITERIA:

Keyword(s):

Opportunity Number:

CFDA:

SEARCH

OPPORTUNITY STATUS:

☐ Forecasted (325)

☑ Posted (2,471)

☐ Closed (6,229)

☐ Archived (64,462)

▸ FUNDING INSTRUMENT TYPE:

▸ ELIGIBILITY:

▸ CATEGORY:

▸ AGENCY:

Figure 4.2: Federal search options

SEARCH NOTES:

- Click the *Search* button (shown in *Figure 4.2*) without entering a keyword to generate a comprehensive search hit list (on right of the screen) of all the current and pending solicitations. If you do have a specific topic in mind, put in the keyword before clicking *Search*.

- Once you have clicked *Search* (either with or without a keyword), you can filter gradually by selecting or de-selecting options.

- Some keywords will be more productive than others, so do a few keyword searches before filtering any of them.

- In the "Eligibility" drop list, choose the *Unrestricted* checkbox at the bottom of that list together with any other check boxes appropriate to your eligibility (e.g., *Private institutions of higher education*). Then, you will find the largest number of solicitations that may align with your interests.

- Start broadly. Even NSF has some humanities and social science solicitations, generally combined with science or technology in some way.

- In the "Agency" options section, for those new to the process, initially leave *All Agencies* checked as you conduct your preliminary search. You can subsequently refine your search by selecting individual agencies or other options.

- The column headers at the top of the search hit list allow you to sort the data by the chosen header.

- You can filter the data by selecting or de-selecting agencies. When you change the agency options the search hit list will update automatically. Do not click the *Search* button again unless you want to reset your entire search.

- When you open the description of a search hit by clicking on its opportunity number, be sure to record the opportunity number itself; that will make it easier to find the solicitation later.

- When ready to start a new search, remove or change the keyword if there is one, and click the *Search* button to clear the previous options and start over.

4.1.2   Example: Federal Solicitation Search

A new biochemistry faculty member interested in funding a climate science project relevant to her research enters the keyword "climate" as her grants.gov basic search criterion and clicks the *Search* button.

There are initially several hundred posted search hits related to climate across all agencies, types, eligibilities and categories. She subsequently narrows the search one option at a time as follows, noting the effect:

- Opportunity status: *Posted* (She de-selects *Forecasted* to focus her search on current solicitations.)
- Funding instrument type: *Grant*
- Eligibility: *Unrestricted, Public and State controlled institutions of higher education,* and *Private institutions of higher education.*

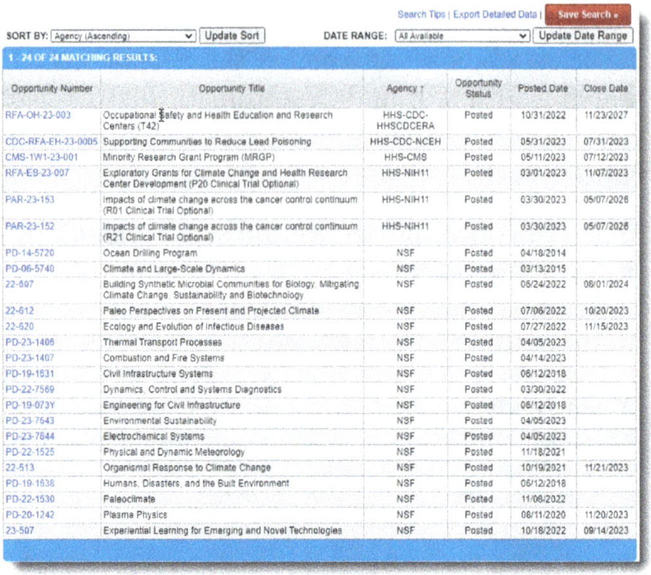

Opportunity Number	Opportunity Title	Agency ↑	Opportunity Status	Posted Date	Close Date
RFA-OH-23-003	Occupational Safety and Health Education and Research Centers (T42)	HHS-CDC-HHSCDCERA	Posted	10/31/2022	11/23/2027
CDC-RFA-EH-23-0005	Supporting Communities to Reduce Lead Poisoning	HHS-CDC-NCEH	Posted	05/31/2023	07/31/2023
CMS-1W1-23-001	Minority Research Grant Program (MRGP)	HHS-CMS	Posted	05/11/2023	07/12/2023
RFA-ES-23-007	Exploratory Grants for Climate Change and Health Research Center Development (P20 Clinical Trial Optional)	HHS-NIH11	Posted	03/01/2023	11/07/2023
PAR-23-153	Impacts of climate change across the cancer control continuum (R01 Clinical Trial Optional)	HHS-NIH11	Posted	03/30/2023	05/07/2026
PAR-23-152	Impacts of climate change across the cancer control continuum (R21 Clinical Trial Optional)	HHS-NIH11	Posted	03/30/2023	05/07/2026
PD-14-5720	Ocean Drilling Program	NSF	Posted	04/18/2014	
PD-06-5740	Climate and Large-Scale Dynamics	NSF	Posted	03/13/2015	
22-607	Building Synthetic Microbial Communities for Biology, Mitigating Climate Change, Sustainability and Biotechnology	NSF	Posted	06/24/2022	08/01/2024
22-612	Paleo Perspectives on Present and Projected Climate	NSF	Posted	07/06/2022	10/20/2023
22-620	Ecology and Evolution of Infectious Diseases	NSF	Posted	07/27/2022	11/15/2023
PD-23-1406	Thermal Transport Processes	NSF	Posted	04/05/2023	
PD-23-1407	Combustion and Fire Systems	NSF	Posted	04/14/2023	
PD-19-1631	Civil Infrastructure Systems	NSF	Posted	06/12/2018	
PD-22-7569	Dynamics, Control and Systems Diagnostics	NSF	Posted	03/30/2022	
PD-19-073Y	Engineering for Civil Infrastructure	NSF	Posted	06/12/2018	
PD-23-7643	Environmental Sustainability	NSF	Posted	04/05/2023	
PD-23-7644	Electrochemical Systems	NSF	Posted	04/05/2023	
PD-22-1525	Physical and Dynamic Meteorology	NSF	Posted	11/18/2021	
22-513	Organismal Response to Climate Change	NSF	Posted	10/19/2021	11/21/2023
PD-19-1638	Humans, Disasters, and the Built Environment	NSF	Posted	06/12/2018	
PD-22-1530	Paleoclimate	NSF	Posted	11/08/2022	
PD-20-1242	Plasma Physics	NSF	Posted	08/11/2020	11/20/2023
23-507	Experiential Learning for Emerging and Novel Technologies	NSF	Posted	10/18/2022	09/14/2023

Figure 4.3: Final filtered search hit list

Initially, there are still several dozen search hits from a variety of government agencies, several of which are out of the scope for her idea. She does see one NEH (National Endowment for the Humanities) solicitation that might have partnership potential, so she makes a note of its opportunity number and title in case she wants to return to it.

Going back to her search hit list, she then clicks the arrow in the *Agency* column header to sort them alphabetically, scans each agency's offerings, and gradually selects several of them using the Agency options box. Finally, only two dozen NSF and HHS solicitations remain. (See *Figure 4.3.*) She clicks several interesting titles to see the full description, and then downloads the three most interesting by clicking the *Export Detailed Data* link, plus the NEH hit she saved, to read the full solicitations.

The search filtering process in this example applies to any and all fields of inquiry, not just STEM. Whether you are looking for a biology or an arts one, you will follow the same procedure.

4.1.3 Federal Search Shortcuts

There are some shortcuts in the search of federal solicitations that are useful.

- Most federal grants are assigned a CFDA number. (See *Chapter 4* glossary). Once you determine the CFDAs common to your area of (e.g. 47.075 is usually associated with "Social, Behavioral, and Economic Sciences" at NSF), you can then use that number to find solicitations in related fields. Search that number in grants.gov with the *Search* button and you get several dozen hits in various social sciences.

- Grants directly to individuals are rare, but there are some. (Most grants go through institutions.) Click the *Search* button without a keyword, and then click *Individual* in the Eligibility option section. Add *Other* eligibility if you do not find anything, and then *Unrestricted* to maximize the number of hits that will even consider an individual proposal. Just remember, the Unrestricted hits will receive both individual and organizational proposals, which makes them even more competitive than usual.

4.2   Foundation Solicitations

Unlike federal grants, there is no single comprehensive search engine for foundation, private, and community grants, and their requirements vary widely, so cast a broad net using multiple grant search engines and strategies. (Examples from different disciplines appear in *Sections 4.2.1 and 4.2.2*.)

4.2.1   Example: Search for a Travel Grant

History projects frequently require travel to review original sources and do certain types of fieldwork. Professor Smith has an idea to research a book project and a new interdisciplinary course on the social and environmental effects of post World War II population growth. A quick search of the NEH on grants.gov produced one possibility that might work: a solicitation on Archaeological and Ethnographic Field Research, but the due date is too soon. He records its opportunity and CFDA numbers for future use and moves on to a different search.

Professor Smith also has access to the Grant Station search engine through his *Chronicle of Philanthropy* subscription. Grant Station has a different interface than grants.gov, as well as a few extra features. (See *Chapter 6* for concept paper storage on Grant Station.)

Smith now clicks *Find Grantmakers* on a top menu bar and initially clicks *Research Process* to familiarize himself with some searching strategies. He then clicks *Find Grantmakers* again to choose the search location; these include US Charitable, US Federal, US State, Canadian Charitable, Canadian Government, and International Charitable.

He begins with US Charitable, which opens a screen with a long search bar. (See *Figure 4.5.*)

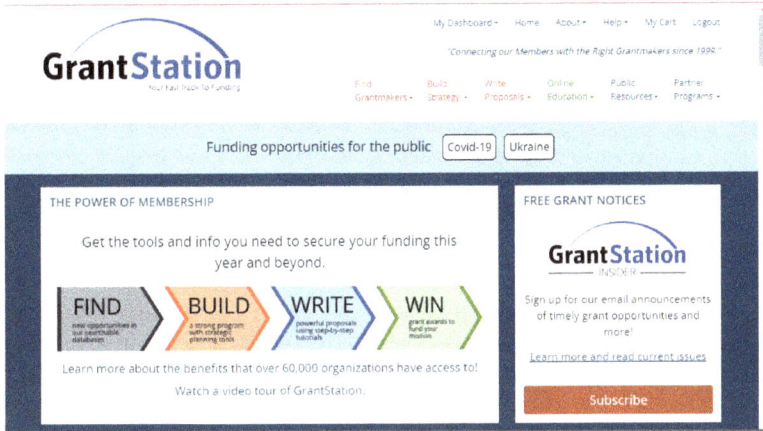

Figure 4.4: Grant Station home page

In general, when using this search bar:

- Choose the geographic scope of the search first.

- Start with a simple search and save promising hits.

- Notice that the hits are granting organizations, not solicitations. You will need to search the granting organization's website for actual solicitations.

- Add keywords only if needed.

- Save searches by name if they have future value. (Unlike federal offerings, private grants do not have a CFDA or an opportunity number.)

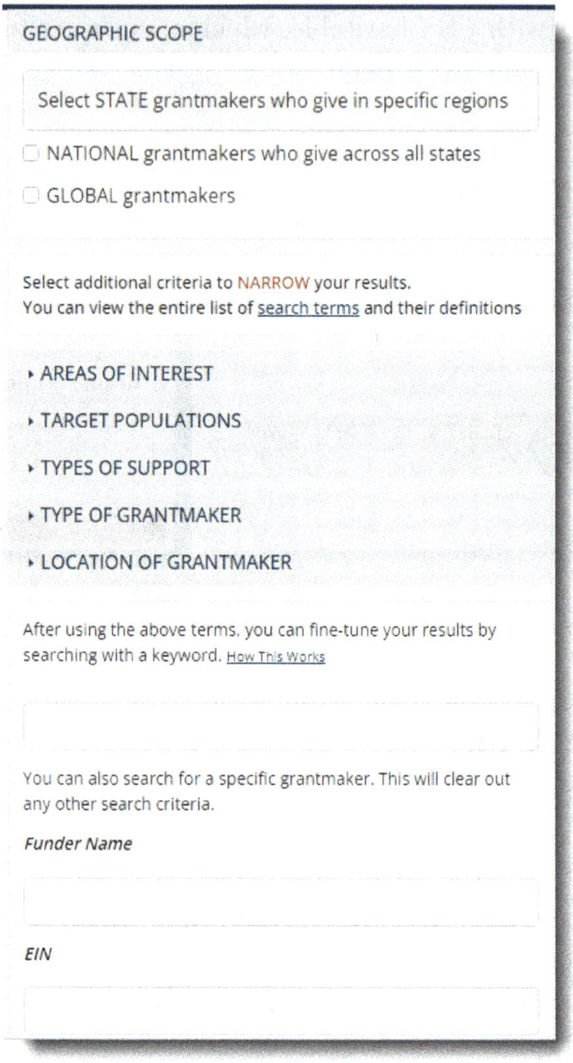

GEOGRAPHIC SCOPE

Select STATE grantmakers who give in specific regions

☐ NATIONAL grantmakers who give across all states

☐ GLOBAL grantmakers

Select additional criteria to NARROW your results.
You can view the entire list of search terms and their definitions

▸ AREAS OF INTEREST

▸ TARGET POPULATIONS

▸ TYPES OF SUPPORT

▸ TYPE OF GRANTMAKER

▸ LOCATION OF GRANTMAKER

After using the above terms, you can fine-tune your results by searching with a keyword. How This Works

You can also search for a specific grantmaker. This will clear out any other search criteria.

Funder Name

EIN

Figure 4.5: Grant Station search bar

Because Professor Smith's project is interdisciplinary, there is unlikely to be a grant tailor-made for it, so he keeps the search wide open. He constructs a search with only the following criteria: *US National scope* and *travel expenses* (from the "Types of Support" drop list).

This produces four pages of hits, and he scans through them one at a time, saving two that look promising.

- American Historical Society: the Albert J. Beveridge Grant for Research into the History of the Western Hemisphere. Specifically a travel grant for finishing existing projects in any aspect of Western Hemisphere history.

- Gladys Krieble Delmas Foundation: Humanities program. This includes history and "...welcomes projects that cross the boundaries between humanistic disciplines and explore the connection between the humanities and other areas of scholarship."[3]

There were two additional leads that would require a different slant on the idea and a partner from another discipline (Journalism and Psychology, respectively), so Professor Smith saves those as well.

4.2.2 Example : Search for a Visiting Scholar Grant

Professor Habig chairs a fledgling dance program with only two full-time non-tenure track faculty members. She would like to hire a visiting faculty member in the field. Initially

---

[3]delmas.org/programs-for-organizations

she does a quick Google search and sifts through several pages of links. Some are off-topic, on suspension, or specific to dance companies.

She does find several promising links, in addition to some background information on dance and health:

- a good blog post on finding dance grants through networking and collaboration:
  blog.daisie.com/10-effective-ways-to-find-grants-for-your-dance-program

- a link to a free InstrumentL page of foundations supporting dance
  instrumentl.com/browse-grants/grants-for-dance-nonprofit-organizations

  and two grants from that dance page:

    - O'Donnell-Green Music and Dance Foundation Grant (residency in a few states)
      odonnellgreen.com

    - Shubert Foundation Dance Grants
      shubertfoundation.org/dance

- an NEA page entitled "Grants for Arts Projects: Dance"
  arts.gov/grants

- an NEA list of state and regional arts organizations that may have grants
  arts.gov/state-and-regional-arts-organizations

- a search hit list at grants.gov with the term "visiting scholar," constrained by agency to NEH.

After a thorough perusal of these materials, and changing the search term a couple of times, it becomes clear that a straightforward visiting professor salary is less likely to get funding than something more innovative. She considers how linking two organizations might push collaboration to partnership, with dual hiring, sharing resources and expenses. This partnership might enable funding for a hybrid performance/teaching/research project: one with a public health colleague, or with a local non-profit dance organization, or another with a media company.

PRACTICE THIS: Evaluating Hits

Whether or not you have an idea for a grant, conduct some searches at grants.gov and other search engines to get comfortable with the process. Use different search terms: in the dance example, the professor changed terms several times and this helped her build a more fundable proposal.

- Do one or more grants align with your project? Or does an interesting solicitation spur some thinking?

- How can you adapt your fundable proposal to the specific solicitation?

- Did you search database archives to learn what has already been funded in your area?

- Are the promising solicitations you found a good fit with your proposal's three-merit criteria? (See *Section 3.2.*)

- What deliverables are required?

- Would your project be more fundable with a partnership?

- Will the grant pay for equipment? Student stipends? Other expenses?

- Will you have the option to renew?

Chapter 5

Working with Others

Collaborations and Partnerships

Academic inquiry often requires collaboration or partnerships. It can be as straightforward as two members of one discipline teaming up on a project or multiple disciplines working together. Collaboration can entail not only internal scholarly teamwork at the same institution, but also external partnerships with nonprofits, other institutions of higher learning, local governing boards, or industry. Some solicitations encourage collaboration and partnerships; this can be advantageous to smaller institutions.

Chapter 5 Glossary

- **Partnership:** In grant development, the term refers to the working relationship between two or more organizations to propose and complete a specific project. Each entity contributes knowledge, time, ideas, resources, and work, and shares in the results.[1] For the purposes of this book, partnerships will typically be external.

- **Collaboration:** Distinct from partnership, collaboration indicates that other schools or organizations support and participate in the program but not necessarily share its administrative responsibilities. For this purposes of this book, collaboration will typically occur within individual institutions or informally among multiple institutions.

- **Unwritten Rules:** Undocumented procedures and practices that govern who to talk to and in what order (essentially etiquette specific to the institution).

5.1   Advantages

There are substantial advantages to both collaboration and partnerships. A distributed workload is more time-efficient for all partners. Multiple voices can lead to a more innovative set of ideas. External partnerships, particularly for smaller institutions, provide greater resources and facilities, a larger network, and expanded expertise. In short, they

---

[1] Adapted from the IRS definition of a business partnership.

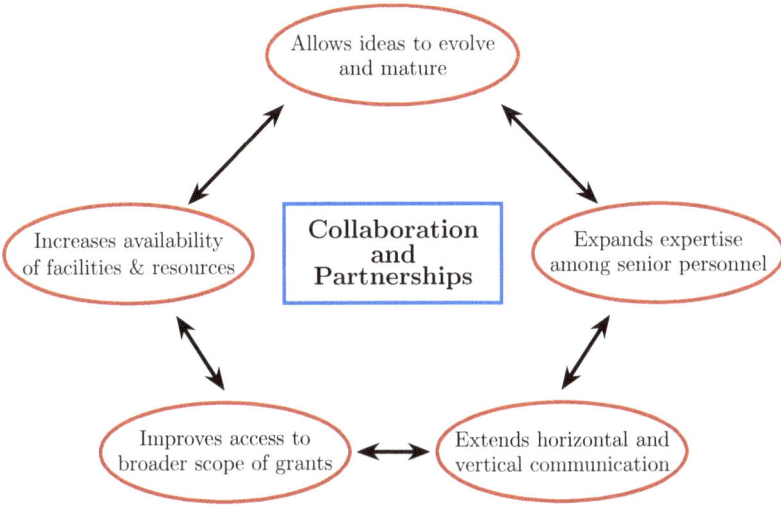

Figure 5.1: Advantages of collaboration and partnerships

make proposals from smaller colleges or universities more competitive on more complex grants.

Scholars can be hesitant about collaboration and partnerships of any kind for a number of reasons. It may be difficult to sell a proposal idea to people they don't know very well. Or they may wonder how to get started, feel that they lack required skills, and be concerned about having the time to coordinate deadlines with others. (See *Section 5.2* if there are concerns around idea security.)

Get to know the research/scholarship support infrastructure at your institution, from library subscriptions to the Grants Office. Know where to find relevant Human Resources policies (e.g. visa sponsorships for visiting scholars, background checks if minors will be on campus, and so on).

If new at collaborative projects, start small. Some grants are easier to write and administer. A successful first run can support future attempts to take on more complex collaborations.

Success requires trustworthy partners, diverse points of view, and good management right from the beginning.

- Assign the lead on each section of the grant development to individual team members: budget, narrative, references, etc.

- Listen, negotiate, and adapt as new ideas arise, while at the same time documenting everything.

- Maintain a flexible timeline with specific expectations and goals, but also room for change.

- Keep in touch with everyone, especially those participating remotely.

- Be alert for times when initial enthusiasm starts to wane, and ask for suggestions.

5.2   Safeguarding Ideas

In our workshops, many voices note that they fear their proposal ideas might be stolen, which highlights the need for trust before and during a proposal project. Get to know potential team members before allowing them onboard, and share with them only after discussing how and when you expect anyone else to know details. Avoid broadcasting a proposal idea widely until it is well documented and copies have been distributed to the administration.

It takes time to build a trusted network, and although feedback is crucial, be careful. There are no guarantees, and copyrighting an idea by itself is not possible, but there are ways to manage control of it.

5.2.1 Team Dynamics

As a team works on an idea, it is very likely to evolve in new directions. Discussion and change are healthy for idea development, but be on guard when brainstorming. Ownership is a sticky subject. Listening and respect can ensure that ownership overall remains with the team, while still acknowledging each person's contribution. Guarantee that the colleague who first voices an idea retains its attribution. Everyone needs to trust everyone else. Be certain to speak up and credit the originator of an idea, even as it changes. ("Well, as Joan noted at the beginning,...") This is particularly important if someone else on the team, more vocal than others, begins to claim personal ownership of someone else's contribution.

5.2.2 Document and Communicate When Ready

It takes time to build a trusted network. The biggest danger of idea theft occurs when it is not immediately actionable. Keep a research diary to record dates and times of conversations, the idea's originator, and other data on what the team did and when they did it. Take care where, how, and with whom you share ideas that have not yet been documented or attributed to the team. One way to ensure attribution is to copy the grants officer or administrator on all communications and follow up on all conversations, and document those conversations as well.

5.3   Internal Collaboration

The first step in working with colleagues is to become familiar with your own institution's policies and practices, which can help convince potential collaborators to come on board. Get to know fellow researchers in various disciplines and venues, whether on committees, in interdisciplinary teaching opportunities, campus theater productions, or just chatting at lunch. Some colleagues may demonstrate interest in collaborative grant development work. Find out who on campus has grant experience and contact them for advice. Invite the administration's grant officer to speak or give a workshop.

Besides having a development office or grant coordinator, many administrations offer other kinds of support for grant development. Find out if there are helpful benefits for grant writing (release time, tenure package component, etc.). A provost or dean may fund speakers, create a grants working group to support faculty writing grants, or mediate a discussion of the different ways to understand a research project. If your institution belongs to a consortium of colleges, ask what resources and networking opportunities are available.

One suggested activity is a version of "speed dating," in which participants interested in grant development rotate through brief (5-10 minute) meetings with each other to brainstorm project ideas that might work jointly. The best outcomes happen when the administration organizes and promotes the event by setting up a festive atmosphere with snacks and a general get-to-know-you discussion, with a minimum of speeches ahead of time. Invite some of the staff who will be involved in any grant, and can explain the details of protocols and procedures.

5.4 External Partnerships

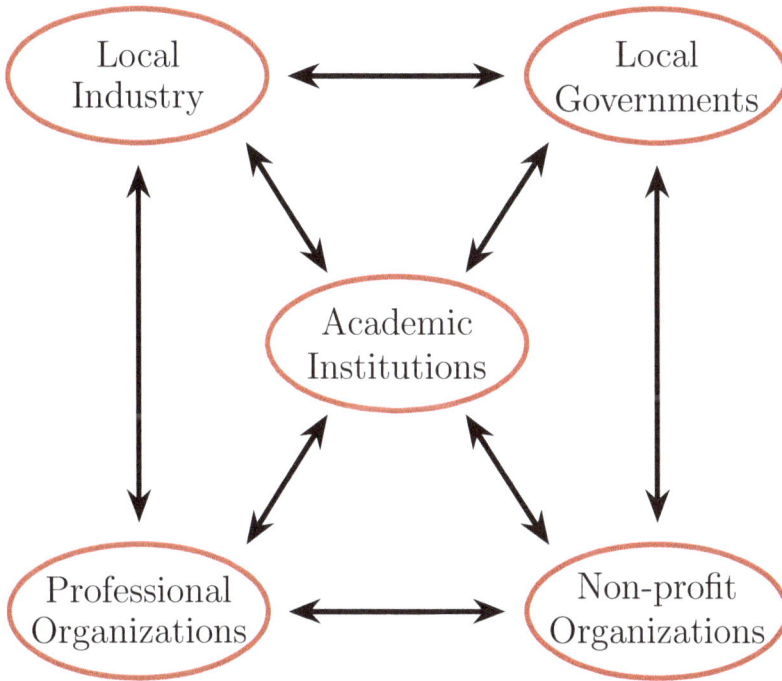

Figure 5.2: The partnership network

Grants with many moving parts often require external partnerships, and while these are advantageous to the individuals and institutions, they come with their own caveats. Benefits can be rewarding, however, building relationships with external partners takes time and effort:

- Budgets require more thought about how funds are distributed, and must document costs for multiple parties.

- Potential partners may already have a relationship with your institution, which you do not want to complicate, so contact the development office, but also other offices that communicate with outside organizations before contacting the potential partner.

- Depending on the institution, offices with external contacts (Career Services, Community Engagement, Communications, Continuing Education, or an Entrepreneurial Office) can help locate potential partners.

- All institutions have procedures and practices, many unwritten, about who to talk to and in what order. Ignore these practices at your peril. Work up the chain of command: usually department chair first, then the development office, then some hierarchy of Dean, Provost, Committee chairs, and others. Learn details on how the institution operates; staff members are often the most knowledgeable about how the offices work, and they are generally very helpful.

- Ongoing communication is key. Once lines of communication are in place, keep all the critical parties continuously informed, calm, and positive about the proposal effort.

PRACTICE THIS: Expensive Resources

A geology professor is preparing a proposal for his research through the NSF Young Investigator program. It requires a scanning electron microscope to visualize crystal structure, but his institution does not have one. Before requesting the funds for this resource in the proposal, he must eliminate the possibility that a nearby university has the same equipment and time to share it.

Think of a (probably expensive) resource that you need for your scholarly work, but lack funds or space to procure. Take into account whether the resource is available at a nearby institution.

How will you construct the proposal...

- to partner with the other institution if the resource is available there?

- if the resource is not available at the other institution, but they are interested in partnering on the proposal?

Chapter 6

The Concept Paper

A Communication Instrument

A **concept paper** is a condensed summary of a potential grant proposal. Having one of these ready helps clarify, support, and focus the eventual proposal to the funding agencies' objectives. It is essentially a sales pitch. Use one to:

- consider all aspects of the project carefully
- introduce the project to colleagues and other stakeholders
- obtain feedback from trusted colleagues
- help transform a good idea into a focused, high-quality proposal

As a best practice, start a folder or database of concept papers to capture ideas for future use. These early drafts do not have to be complete or even have an identified solicitation, but having them on file will provide you with a head start in multiple directions.

Chapter 6 Glossary

- **Concept paper:** A document that captures the idea for a potential grant proposal and gets continually updated as new information becomes available.

- **Institutional Review Board (IRB)** A committee or other administrative body designated to review and monitor all research conducted at an institution.

- **Idea fixation:** Refusing to allow an initial grant idea to evolve into something more targeted, complex, or fundable is counterproductive. Idea fixation blinds you to potential opportunities.

- **Literature review:** The process of investigating, evaluating, assessing, and distilling the relevance of key sources that contribute to the project.

6.1   Overview

Input from various people can help better fit the concept into the area outlined in the solicitation and to the institutional mission. Additionally, feedback on the concept paper will provide guidance on how to address weaknesses and bolster strengths.

During preliminary brainstorming, outreach, and meetings, keep and organize dated notes into a draft that begins building a program design to complement the idea, consistent with vision and goals. Tell your story effectively. Demonstrate how the project aligns with the priorities and mission of the funding agency. Give the reader the ability to evaluate the ideas. Remember, most importantly, this is a living document; add and subtract as proposal development continues, enhanced with new information and comments.

Consider drafting two separate versions of the concept paper, particularly if the proposal team is interdisciplinary. One version targets research colleagues, and can include jargon and technical language. The second version should avoid jargon because it is for administrators, potential sponsors, collaborators, and others outside the field who might have an interest in the concept but not know the technical language.

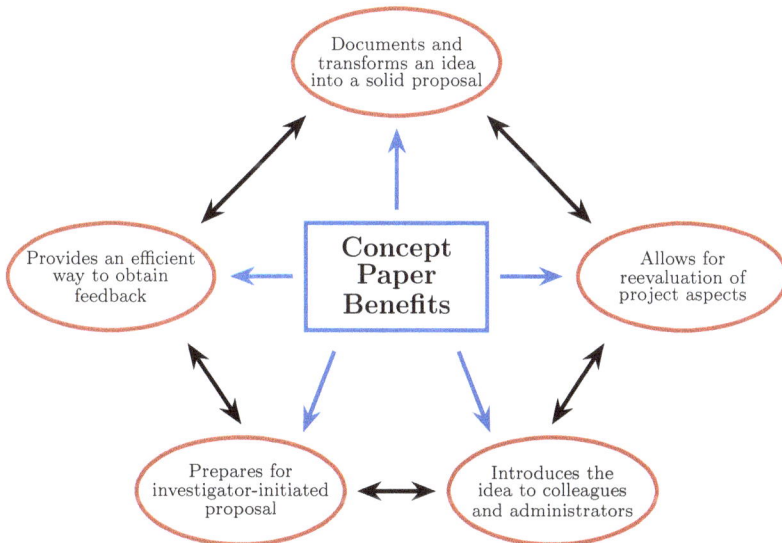

Figure 6.1: Making the most of a concept paper

Online Storage for Concept Papers

If you have access to the Grant Station search engine, you can create and save details of multiple potential projects in their dashboard with descriptions, budget items, and selections from many dozen checkbox options in various categories; this essentially prepares and stores a concept paper for each idea online. (See *Section 3.4* for more.)

6.2   The Proposal's Core Concepts

Before the writing begins, think clearly about what the proposed funding will do. This can be scattershot at the beginning, just brief ideas grouped around three main questions:

1. How will the funded project make a substantial difference or contribution to any or all of the following?

(a) to a body of knowledge,

(b) to a societal issue,

(c) to a specific community,

(d) to the mission of your home institution.

2. Is the argument convincing, logical, and supported well?

3. Are there sufficient resources, facilities, and administrative structures in place to complete the project if and when funding is granted? [1]

Survey scholarly sources both for evidence and to learn the prevailing arguments. How will this project contribute to the debate? Does the project conform to current thinking or does it take any intellectual risks? Does it take an alternative approach? Does it exploit an underused model? Seek out the "novelty" in the idea, with the following caveat: Federal granting agencies want innovation/novelty, but not pie in the sky. Private foundations may even avoid novelty in some cases. Press the preliminary case with clear justifications.

Ensure that the concept aligns with the university mission and resources. Establish performance measures that will clearly indicate the level of success of the funded project. Identify potential outside evaluators (if necessary).

---

[1] This is a fundamental question asked by review panels. It may not seem significant at the outset. However, it is absolutely critical that structural components are in place for the successful administration of any grant.

6.2.1   Importance of Literature Reviews

Be alert! All types of proposals require literature review. The ideation process evolves not just through conversations with your team, but through learning what recent scholarship has preceded your project. Knowing what has been funded and published previously avoids duplication and can influence your project design.

The literature review portion of a grant proposal consists of two interrelated components: start by searching previously funded projects, then follow by searching published scholarship. Keeping a fluid interaction between these two elements benefits the ideation process. When initiating your search of previously funded projects, widen your search parameters to include analogous grant topics. Paradoxically, this strategy will eventually help you focus your idea as you to winnow out unrelated material.

In this way, formulating a grant proposal differs from preparing articles for peer-reviewed journals. Specifically, the review should be focused rather than exhaustive. Instead of final justification for your work, it should be viewed as an extension of the ideation process. It is a tool for sculpting ideas into a fundable project design.

6.3   Institutional Review Board

Under federal regulations[2], the Institutional Review Board (IRB) is a group (committee or administrative body) that

---

[2] "US regulations at 45CFR. 46 subpart E and 21CFR. 56.106 require IRBs to be registered with the DHHS Office of Human Research Protections (OHRP), which is responsible for monitoring compliance with the Common Rule." fda.gov

has been formally designated to review and monitor all research conducted by institution administrators, faculty, and students. In accordance with these regulations, an IRB has the authority to approve, require modifications (to secure approval), or disapprove certain activities, and is mostly used to ensure privacy, humane treatment, and appropriate preparation for human or animal subjects.

There are three general levels of IRB review:

- **Exempt Review** – if proposed research involves no greater than minimal risk to participants. For example, food quality, certain clinical trials, research in which the identity of subjects is not discernable.

- **Expedited Review**—if proposed research involves no greater than minimal risk to participants, but does not meet any of the Exempt categories. Examples include collection of voice data, and some REU and RUI programs.

- **Full Review** – if research does not qualify as exempt or expedited and involves "at risk" subjects or procedures (or data collection) that might cause harm or distress. Examples include: studies involving animals, minors, prisoners, people with diminished mental capacity, or the disadvantaged.

6.4   Collect Documents

Begin to collect documents that you will need. All proposals require a literature review both to demonstrate previous scholarship in the same field and to lend depth to the new idea. It should be complete, but not necessarily total; include results more than five years old only if relevant. Additionally, have ready curricula vitae for team members, a printed out (or easily accessible) copy of the solicitation itself, and a list of potential advisors.

6.5   Concept Paper Template

Concept paper templates are common—hundreds of them are online. This section includes a generic version targeted to grants, easily modifiable for a particular proposal. It is here to get things started. Even without an identified solicitation or other details, it documents thinking and possibilities; change it as needed. Keeping a folder of draft concept papers will help streamline future proposal development. Start one even if you only have a couple of summary sentences for a new idea.

Concept papers should be as concise as possible, at most two pages; although notes to yourself can go on a third page not disseminated widely. The working title, PI name, college name, and contact information belong in a heading. When completed, the project background, purpose, and description should take up about half the total length. All the other sections should be approximately a paragraph each.

6.5.1   Summary

Briefly summarize (1) the significant question, problem, or gap the proposal will address and why it is important; (2) the expected outcome(s); and (3) the potential broader impact. The summary should be particularly persuasive regarding the project's significance and impact so as to grab the audience and keep them reading. Include language from the solicitation and demonstrate understanding of the targeted funding agency's strategic priorities so that program officers see their organization reflected in the project and notes how the project advances its cause.

6.5.2   Background and Purpose

Convince the funding agency that:

- the proposer is knowledgeable about the research topic,

- more research is necessary to fill in the gaps, expand upon the literature, or address critical problems,

- the project design will meet the promises and answer the questions presented in the proposal,

- the project matters and is both significant and timely to the funding agency's priorities and the body of knowledge in the field.

Start with a clear, concise description of the research *topic* (not the actual project—that's the next section). Include a brief summary of pivotal literature to provide context, and highlight if there is little or no research directly aligned with the project. Avoid both hyperbole and minutiae.

6.5.3   Project Description

Concisely describe your research project, including:

- what you plan to do, how you plan to do it (methodology, data collection, analysis),

- who is involved and who will benefit (directly and indirectly),

- innovative aspects of the research approach that set your project apart from others,

- research questions, goal(s) and objectives,

- the timeline and major milestones for what the project accomplishes,

- expected outcomes of the project, linked to research questions/goals, in terms of its impact on the target population and alignment with the funding agency goals.

6.5.4   Costs, Dates, and Key Personnel

Think carefully about what expenses are included and why. Find out what things cost and use that as evidence. Include an estimate of total costs (direct and indirect—see *Section 7.3.3*), categories of expenses, and the project time-frame (start/end dates). Discuss your qualifications as PI and the expertise of your team as a whole. Do not include a detailed budget; that is for the full proposal.

6.5.5 Project Impact

This section reaffirms the importance of your project to the funding agency's mission. Briefly restate why the project is important, its expected outcomes, its impacts on all targets, how it will add new knowledge to the field, and how it reflects the funding agency's strategic priorities.

6.5.6 References

References are not necessary for a concept paper, but have them ready should anyone wish to see them.

PRACTICE THIS: Arts and Humanities

You have an idea to honor the culture and legacy of Indigenous American artists by recording their stories as part of an exhibition you are organizing for a broader Arts community. Small grants are available through the National Performance Network (NPN) *Creation Fund to Advance Racial and Cultural Justice through the Arts.*[a] This solicitation "provides a framework for relationships to develop, over time, among diverse artists, arts organizations, and communities." NPN encourages relationships among artists and organizations. To this end, the solicitation you are applying for supports new work with three criteria as shown on their website:

- Apply to the Fund with at least two other organizations (co-commissioners) led by an NPN National Partner.

- Each commissioner contributes a $2,000 - $3,000 cash match and agrees to present the created work.

- NPN matches these funds so that every rewarded artist receives at least $14,000 for their project.

Construct a concept paper that fits the solicitation criteria.

---

[a]npnweb.org/programs/cdf/

Chapter 7

Draft a Budget

Follow the Money

The budget design process is a good way to identify specific funding needs for the project during proposal development. Create a draft budget early in order to match the configuration of the project to the available funds. Additionally, an early budget can help structure how records will be kept and determine the commitment level of internal and external partners. This draft will continuously change as the proposal develops. Allied with a convincing concept paper, a detailed budget helps transform a good idea into a focused, high-quality proposal.

Chapter 7 Glossary

- **Budget justification:** A short narrative that explains the reasons for including specific costs in the project budget.

- **Direct costs:** That portion of a project's budget that goes directly toward execution of the project's activities.

- **Indirect costs:** That portion of a project's budget that supports the project's administration, but which is not directly attributable to support of project activities.

- **An allowable cost:** A cost borne by the grant that is deemed reasonable by both the funding agency and home institution, and constitutes what a prudent person might pay.

- **An allocable cost:** A cost necessary in the project budget based on the benefit the cost provides to the project.

- **Senior personnel (SP):** These include the PI, co-PIs, and any other project executive that contributes to the implementation, execution, or development of a project in a substantive, quantifiable way, regardless of whether they are compensated financially under the grant.

- **Participants:** Individuals who are recipients (not producers) of the services or opportunities provided by the project's activities.

- **NICRA (Negotiated Indirect Cost Rate Agreement):** This agreement documents the negotiated institutional indirect and fringe benefit cost rate between the Federal Government and the Grantee's organization. It identifies the ratio between some direct cost base and the total indirect expenses an organization should bear. (It should be publicly accessible.)

7.1 Overview

Federal, state, and private foundation funding sources have different requirements for the content and format of proposal budgets; however, all of them want thorough, reportable, and traceable documentation. Moreover, your institution has its own budgetary policies and procedures. Both sets of requirements matter. Be aware of institutional restrictions, too, and coordinate with all offices that will handle funds. Approval for spending grant funds may require more signatures than just the principal investigator's. These can include administrators, financial officers, grants officers, and those responsible for purchases. Determine early on who will need to approve and monitor funding for your project.

For an awarded grant, the administrators responsible for expense approval should keep an accounting record of what has been spent and what funds remain. Even if accounts payable keeps records, we highly recommend that the PI also keep a complete record of all expenditures (how much, to whom, when it was spent, what category, etc.) with notes that reflect the reasons for the expense. The PI should always know the balance on the account and make decisions based on what funds are available.

The budget template sample in *Section 7.4* lists common, customizable components useful as you pursue specific solicitations. Using a spreadsheet, updated regularly, will help handle planning contingencies and allow easily modifiable estimates during proposal development. These spreadsheets often include more detail than goes into the final proposal (the NSF/NIH only want category totals, for example, not specific instances from those categories), but having that detail helps keep track of everything. It also helps grants officers at your home institution who upload the final budget during the grant submission process.

The funding agency and in some cases the applicant institution determine matters such as allowable expenses, any applicable funding salary caps, overhead (Facilities and Administration), and other budgetary matters. College and university grants officers do not and cannot make these determinations for Federal and many other funding agencies. Notify your grants office (or appropriate administrator) when you intend to apply for active solicitations so that they will be prepared to assist you with budgetary questions. (In some cases they may be able to provide their own spreadsheet template.)

Keep budget details, spreadsheets, and justification documents secure. Some budgetary information is sensitive; collaborators/partners may not want salaries or other information publicly available. Senior personnel privy to this information should honor its sensitivity. Some important concepts are described below.

7.2 Budget Justification

This statement is vital. It explains in detail how the proposal meets the funding agency's specific requirements. It justifies the research project costs, validates and explains the importance of the requested expenditures and is another opportunity to sell the project. Explain in detail what the project will spend and why those expenses should be included. For example, "Dr. Flowers, lead investigator and PI, will direct and oversee all aspects of the proposed project, including x, y, and z. Dr. Flowers will spend three calendar months on this project."

Make certain that you align the justification statement with the budget, and that all budgetary items are described and accounted for within the justification. This alignment should demonstrate a thorough conceptual understanding of the proposed project. The budget and the justification statement must be in complete harmony, and consistent with the overall manuscript. Any discrepancy may reduce reviewer confidence in the proposal.

7.3 Allowable Project Costs

Both the funding agency and the institution will have regulations on allowable expenses. These regulations may differ. Find out in advance what is and is not an allowable expense by both the agency and your home institution. This information may be accessible online. For example, if a participant's car breaks down while conducting a project activity, the car repair is not an allowable expense. However, parking expenses for that car are allowable.

Things to consider include:

- Some funding agencies (e.g., Dept. of Defense) may request breakouts of health care benefits for students or postdocs supported in part on other Federal grants. Your grants officer can investigate this.

- Some funding agencies request salary information be split into salary and benefits; others require a projected annual salary increase for employees.

- Your grants officer can assist with identifying allowable expenses, such as participant cash payments or gift cards, speaker honoraria, lunches for project participants, etc.

- Allowable materials will depend on the nature of the proposed project, but can include everything from lab glassware to art supplies to computers or special-use software licenses. The funding agency will specify categories and provide examples of allowable expenses.

- Read the solicitation with care when considering a large-equipment expense. The funding agency or solicitation often has a hard limit for such cost. Sometimes they issue separate solicitations for large-item purchases, renovations, or new structures. When big-ticket items are excluded from the solicitation, but necessary for the project, ask if there are alternative funding opportunities.

- The approximate value of in-kind support such as donated supplies can be noted in the budget justification.

- Other possible expenses include publication fees, data

dissemination costs, travel expenses, subscription expenses, patent application or filing fees, specialized software licenses, website hosting costs, etc.

7.3.1 Additional Budgetary Suggestions

It is important to coordinate and work closely with your grants office when constructing the budget. Moreover, there are agency-specific budget guides, e.g., the NSF's Proposal and Award Policies and Procedures Guide (PAPPG). These documents supply valuable information that explains how the specific agency wants expenses to be budgeted and what is allowable.

There are also myriad atypical budgetary items that occur infrequently. Here are two examples:

- If a second institutional site is included as a partner or collaborator in the proposal, it may need to provide their own budget and justification statement, as well as their own follow-up reports to the agency.

- If a marketable product is a potential outcome of grant activities, additional budgetary items could include attorney fees, patent application/filing fees, initial production fees, etc.

If there is a question about budget elements for which the solicitation does not specify, and you are uncertain, first ask mentors and colleagues for advice. It is also possible to contact the funding agency for answers. It is always better to ask than to submit incorrect information.

7.3.2   Spending Criteria and Limitations

Both funding agencies and academic institutions will have criteria on how funds should be spent in support of the project (and only the project). The PI should rigorously adhere to these guidelines, recognize that they may differ—even among solicitations from the same agency—and work to resolve any discrepancies. Remember, they will *not* list what is unacceptable, only what is acceptable. Stick to what you have justified and the funding agency has accepted:

- **Avoid anything outside of the "allowable" list**, which includes only accepted costs in your budget and budget justification. For example, put a specific ending date and time for your project, and do not pay for any cost incurred after that ending date and time. If you have accommodations for some participants, make certain you cover that in your budget justification so that it falls under "allowable."

- **Disperse salary increases across the life of the grant.** Some funding agencies cap the income amount senior personnel can receive from the grant, or require annual salary increases be distributed across the life of the grant resulting in identical annual budgets (see *Table 7.2*).

- **Spend out the grant during the allotted time.** This is important. Because funding agencies are required to distribute a certain amount, returning unspent funds presents them with difficulties. Some funding agencies allow for the project to be extended with permission under extenuating circumstances, but be aware of extension deadlines. In general, funding agencies do not look favorably on continually extending the life of a grant just because funds have not been spent out. It is sometimes possible to get a one-year extension, perhaps, but more than that may affect how future proposals are reviewed.

- **Avoid padding the budget, but be ready to adjust it.** It is common practice that, if a proposal is approved for funding, the funding agency may ask you to do it for less money. Have some cost-cutting alternatives ready just in case (fewer conferences, trips, participants, etc). Do not put the cost-cutting suggestions in the proposal itself, but have them in your notes so you are prepared to compromise if necessary.

- **A large budget is allowable, as long as the budget is commensurate with the project.** It may cost more to have a strong team with name recognition, or an extra person. Having the right team in place is critical to project success and the budget should reflect this. Take into account inflationary issues, such as pay raises over multiple years. Again, do not pad, but put what you think you need for success.

- **Research what things cost, and document those costs.** Have your team provide details and alternatives. Be frugal. Collect estimates from multiple vendors for high-cost items such as hotels and meals. (The institution may require multiple bids. However, the funding agency usually does not require those details.) Research into allowable expenses helps when writing the budget justification.

- **Follow funding agency guidelines to the letter.**
  Funding agencies often publish guides with instructions, but policies change. Follow the most recent issue of the solicitation or agency documents (e.g., NSF's Proposal and Award Policies and Procedures Guide—PAPPG).

ALLOWABLE EXPENSES:

Grant budgets can be structured so that participants are reimbursed for expenses generated by their involvement in the project or the grant pays for participant expenses directly. Some examples follow:

Expenses that **are** allowable:

- If the grant is structured to reimburse participants, the following are allowable:

  - Meals that take place during the event. The host institution may place per diem restrictions on meals.

  - Airport meals for the participant while traveling to the event.

  - Hotel rooms from the night prior to the start of the event through the night of the final day of the event, allowing participants to travel the day before and leave the day after the event.

  - Mileage to and from the event only, rate determined by the host institution.

- If the grant is structured to pay for costs directly, the following are allowable:

  – Meals during the event planned by the organizers, who should contact participants ahead of time to determine dietary restrictions.

  – A block of hotel rooms reserved for participants.

  – Mileage to and from the event only, rate determined by the host institution.

Expenses that **are not** allowable:

- If the grant is structured to reimburse participants, the following are not allowable:

  – Any meal expense in excess of the per diem.

  – Meals for family members or other traveling companions not attending the event.

  – Any additional hotel night stays after the final night of the event.

  – Additional hotel rooms for family or traveling companions.

  – Car repairs while traveling to/from the event.

- If the grant is structured to pay for costs directly, the following are not allowable:

  – Meals purchased by participants during the event (if organizers asked about dietary restrictions and provided appropriate meals, eating elsewhere is not a reimbursable expense).

- Additional hotel rooms for family or traveling companions.

- Car repairs while traveling to/from the event.

REASONABLE EXPENSES:

Expenses charged to grant accounts must not only be allowable, they must be reasonable. Some examples follow.

Expenses that **are** reasonable:

- Institutions may require the PI to collect bids from several vendors.

  - For example, if a block of hotel rooms is to be ordered for participants, the PI may need bids from three or four hotels.

  - If reasonable arguments can be given (hotel location, size and availability of rooms), the PI could justify accepting a bid that is not the lowest.

Expenses that **are not** reasonable:

- Expenses covered by other sources, even if allowed by the solicitation, are not reasonable.

  - For example, if a nature preserve has an endowed fund for the maintenance of trails, it is not reasonable to request such funds in a proposal.

  - If daycare is already provided by the institution for the children of participants, daycare cannot be included as part of the grant budget.

7.3.3 Direct vs. Indirect Costs

Most federal solicitations allow for both direct and indirect costs, although other solicitations may not allow the indirect ones. Private foundations have various processes, and do things differently than the federal agencies. Some allow indirect costs, but not an indirect rate, and some do not allow any indirect costs.

- **Direct costs** are budgetary expenses that go toward executing the project itself, e.g. participants' travel expenses (including housing and meals if needed) and their stipends, as well as any supplies essential to the project activities.

- **Indirect costs** are expenses for operating and administering the grant. Grants put a burden on the college; there are staffing, facilities, and other internal expenses. Additionally, the team of senior personnel on the grant are considered administrators, not participants, so their grant salaries, fringe benefits, travel expenses, etc., are indirect. The PI administers both the direct and indirect costs for the grant.

- **Indirect cost <u>rate</u>** refers to the percentage of costs that covers college expenses for project administration. This rate is also referred to as Facilities and Administration. Every institution negotiates its rate with the federal government. This rate varies dramatically from one college to another. [1]

---

[1] "...a device for determining fairly and conveniently within the boundaries of sound administrative principles, what proportion of indirect cost each program should bear." hud.gov/sites/documents/OHC_ICR020216.PDF

For a federal grant, each institution will have a Negotiated
Indirect Cost Rate Agreement (NICRA) with the government. An institution decides which budgetary items consti-
tute indirect costs and what rate is charged. It notifies the
government of its decisions, which are then reflected in the
NICRA. Note that colleges and universities differ widely on
calculating both indirect cost items and indirect cost rate.

Example

For a federal proposal to a Department of Education solicitation that has a $500,000 cap:

1. Get all the the grant costs together and then—paying
   attention to the institution's NICRA—divide them
   into execution (direct) and administration (indirect)
   costs.

   Initially the requested direct costs (for this example)
   are $400,000 and the indirect costs are $100,000.

2. Calculate the percentage of the total indirect cost using the rate from the NICRA (for this example assume
   30%, although for many colleges it will be higher);
   **this is the dollar amount the grant budget must
   pay the college itself.**

   30% of $100,000 is $30,000

3. (Here is where it gets tricky.) Add the above dollar
   amount to the indirect costs for a total of $130,000.

4. The total of direct and indirect is now above $500,000,
   so subtract the $30,000 from the direct costs to bring

the total back to $500,000.

5. The grant will now only fund direct costs of $370,000, so adjust the direct cost expenses in the budget to accommodate this deduction. (See *Section 7.3.2* for additional limitations and potential adjustments.)

6. The $30,000 will be refunded to the institution, and it decides what to do with the funds. Some keep it for other projects, some return it to the PI or the department so they they can hire staff (administrative assistants, adjuncts), add to their travel slush fund, and so on. Ask your grants officer what your institution's policy is.

7.4 Budget/Justification Example

An example of a budget and its justification statement appears below. Required budget elements differ among solicitations: senior personnel wages and fringe benefits, participant costs, consultant services, equipment and materials, etc. For every solicitation, though, clear assignment of labor is critical to proposal and project success. The funding agency wants to know details on the roles for people involved in the project. Some of the questions to address: Who is managing activities? Who is developing material? What prior experience do they have? Remember to justify why and what they are being paid (see *Section 7.2*). This example is designed to give some idea of what budget information could be required.

Example: Shoe-print Project

Dr. Flowers and his forensic colleague Dr. Habib have conjectured that people in disparate regions have different walking habits, suggesting that wear patterns on shoe soles might be distinctive by region. To test their hypothesis, they propose a project that brings together twenty scientists across multiple disciplines to examine data and develop methodologies, procedures and guidelines for analysis of wear patterns. Dr. Flowers and Dr. Habib will be assisted by postdoc Dr. Shanahan, whose research is in digital forensics. Pattern recognition experts will also serve as consultants on the project.

Some budget acronyms and terms appear in Table 7.1 that will be used in the Shoe-print project budget.

Table 7.1: List of acronyms and terms for shoe-print project Budget

Acronym	Explanation
AY	One academic-year month.
SU	One summer month.
CY	One calendar-year month, either AY or SU.
MTDC	Modified Total Direct Costs.[2]
F and A	Facilities and Administration.[3]

Table 7.2 is an example of the full budget as it would appear for the shoe-print project.

---

[2]The basis for calculating indirect costs for a project. Some institutions cap the total amount of indirect costs, thus the designation "Modified."

[3]This expression is sometimes used instead of "indirect costs."

Table 7.2: Internal budget for shoe-print forensics project.

Budget Item	Year 1	Year 2	Year 3	Total
Senior Personnel				
(two CY/year)				
(3% per year-dispersed)				
Dr. Flowers (PI)	$24,800	$24,800	$24,800	$74,400
Dr. Habib (co-PI)	$16,400	$16,400	$16,400	$49,200
Dr. Shanahan (SP)	$10,000	$10,000	$10,000	$30,000
Other Personnel				
(Salaries & Wages)				
Staff Support	$3,710	$3,710	$3,710	$11,130
Other	$0	$0	$0	$0
Total Salaries	$54,910	$54,910	$54,910	$164,730
Fringe Benefits[4]				
(44.56% AY rate,				
(8.25% SU rate)				
(7.65% FICA/Medicare)				
Dr. Flowers *(1 AY month)*	$6,682	$6,682	$6,682	$20,046
Dr. Flowers *(1 SU month)*	$2,163	$2,163	$2,163	$6,489
Dr. Habib *(1 AY month)*	$4,281	$4,281	$4,281	$12,843
Dr. Habib *(1 SU month)*	$1,386	$1,386	$1,386	$4,158
Dr. Shanahan *(2 SU months)*	$1,690	$1,690	$1,690	$5,070
Staff Support *(1 SU month)*	$627	$627	$627	$1,881
Other	$0	$0	$0	$0
Total Fringe Benefits	$16,829	$16,829	$16,829	$50,487
Total Salaries and Fringe	$71,739	$71,739	$71,739	$215,217
PI/co-PI/Senior Personnel				
Professional Travel				
Domestic	$6,000	$6,000	$6,000	$18,000
International	$0	$0	$0	$0
Total PI Travel	$6,000	$6,000	$6,000	$18,000
Participant Support Costs				
(Total for 20 participants)				
Stipends	$96,000	$96,000	$96,000	$288,000
Travel to/from program	$30,000	$30,000	$30,000	$90,000
Subsistence				
Housing	$30,000	$30,000	$30,000	$90,000
Meals	$10,000	$10,000	$10,000	$30,000
Research Funds	$10,000	$10,000	$10,000	$30,000
			Continued on next page	

[4]A wage supplement covering health insurance and retirement fund contributions.

Table **7.2** – continued from previous page

Budget Item	Year 1	Year 2	Year 3	Total
Total Participant Costs	$176,000	$176,000	$176,000	$528,000
Other Direct Costs				
Publication Costs	$3,000	$3,000	$3,000	$9,000
Consultant Services	$15,000	$15,000	$15,000	$45,000
Computer Services	$0	$0	$0	$0
Subawards	$0	$0	$0	$0
Other	$0	$0	$0	$0
Total Other Direct Costs	$18,000	$18,000	$18,000	$54,000
Other Indirect Costs				
Materials and Supplies	$1,000	$1,000	$1,000	$3,000
Total Other Indirect Costs	$1,000	$1,000	$1,000	$3,000
Total Indirect Costs	$78,739	$78,739	$78,739	$236,217
MTDC Base[5]	$25,000	$25,000	$25,000	$25,000
Indirect Cost Rate (44.5%)	$11,125	$11,125	$11,125	$33,375
Total Budget	$283,864	$283,864	$283,864	$851,592

---

[5]The basis for calculating indirect costs for a project. Some institutions cap the total amount of indirect costs, thus the designation "Modified."

Shoe-print Project Example Continued:

Table 7.3 shows a budget justification statement for the Shoe-print Project example. Explanations of key budget justification components are italicized in parenthetical comments.

Table 7.3: Shoe-print project budget justification

Budget Justification

Senior/Key Personnel

(*Provide clear explanations of responsibilities and time spent on the project for all senior personnel. Begin by stating any regulations or salary requirements.*)

Personnel are subject to a 3% increase per year as per negotiated union contracts.

Dr. Flowers will be the Principal Investigator and Managing Director of the project. He will oversee the work done at ABC College and under the subcontracts to the XYZ College and the City Community Organization. In addition, he will help recruit and work with participants. He will devote at least one academic-year (AY) and one summer (SU) month to each year of the project.

Dr. Habib is a co-PI on the project and Director for Diversity, Equity, and Inclusion at ABC College. She will coordinate consultants, and project activity development. She will devote one academic-year (AY) and one summer (SU) month to each year of the project.

Dr. Shanahan is senior personnel on the project and an expert in digital forensics. She will coordinate the collection, cleaning,

and analysis of data, and establish guidelines for the use of technology. She will devote two calendar (CY) months per year to
this effort.

Fringe Benefits

(*Clearly describe fringe benefits. A table is helpful.*)

Table 7.4: Fringe rate for shoe-print project

	Fringe Rate	FICA/Medicare	Combined
Faculty and Staff	44.56%	7.65%	52.21%
Summer Salary	8.25%	7.65%	16.9%

FICA/Medicare are separated out as direct costs and not part of
the fringe benefits. For awards, FICA/Medicare are specifically
identified by each employee/personnel and charged separately as
a direct cost expense.

Consultant Services

(*Provide clear explanations of the need for, and responsibilities
of, all consultants.*)

A project of this nature requires the input of experts in forensic
pattern recognition, digital forensics, and algorithmic methods.
A description of the planned work for each consultant follows
below. A total of $45,000 over the life of the project is allocated
for consultants.

Sandra Conner of SmartTech Labs will serve as team ad-
visor and coordinator for pattern recognition algorithmic development. She will devote 100 hours at the rate of $75 per hour
to the project, and will receive a yearly payment in the amount
of $7,500.

Shakah Adebayo of Digital Frontiers will serve as lead data analyst, meeting regularly with project participants providing feedback and assessing algorithmic design and effectiveness. He will work 100 hours at the rate of $75 per hour on the project, and will receive a yearly payment in the amount of $7,500.

Travel

(Describe the reasons for travel and who will be covered. This is another place where a table is helpful.)

The travel budget includes, but is not limited to, ground transportation, airfare, hotel accommodations, POV mileage (when applicable), tolls (when applicable), and meals & incidental expenses. The travel budget was derived utilizing historic travel costs. The ABC College budget is estimated as follows:

Table 7.5: Travel budget for shoe-print project

	Year 1	Year 2	Year 3	Total
PI, co-PI, & Sen. Per. to one meeting each year @ $1,000 each	$3,000	$3,000	$3,000	$9,000
PI, co-PI, & Sen. Per. to site workshops, @ $500 each: two each in years 1, 2, and 3.	$3,000	$3,000	$3,000	$9,000
Participants to site workshops @ $500 each participant: two each in years 1, 2, and 3.	$30,000	$30,000	$30,000	$90,000
TOTAL	$36,000	$36,000	$36,000	$108,000

Materials

(Describe the materials, how they will be used, and who will use them.)

Funds totaling $1,000 each in years 1, 2, and 3 will be allocated to provide for necessary materials, storage, and software for project staff and workshop participants.

Sub-awards

(List all organizations who will be participating in the project, their responsibilities, the amount of their sub-award, and how those funds will be spent. Where the project does not have this budget element, it is still useful to include the category with an explanation.)

There are no sub-awards with this project.

Indirect Costs

(Provide the indirect cost, i.e. F&A rate, the date of the current approved NICRA, and what those costs are.)

Indirect costs are budgeted for the on-campus research rate of 44.5% of modified total direct costs (MTDC) pursuant to the negotiated rate agreement between ABC College and the U.S. Department of Health and Human Services (approved 2/15/2022). In this proposal, MTDC therefore includes all costs except for subaward costs over $25,000.

PRACTICE THIS: An Arts & Humanities Project

At the end of Chapter 6 you developed a concept paper for an exhibition that will include a project to honor the legacy of Indigenous American artists. You are seeking a grant from the National Performance Network (NPN). As with many foundations, NPN funds are not intended to cover the entire cost of the event. For that you will need to seek other funding (registration fees, additional donors, etc.). The solicitation outlines what NPN will cover:

- Travel expenses for invited speakers and artists

- Meals to be served to participants

- Event space costs

- Consumable materials and equipment

Draw up a budget that will cover NPN's allowable expenses for their portion of the event.

Chapter 8

Write, Review, Submit

The Narrative

For solicitations that limit proposals to only a few pages, a concept paper may be close to the final document, and only require small changes to meet the funding agency's requirements. For longer proposals (e.g., most federal ones), the concept paper provides a head start on the narrative (see *Section 8.2*). The Workspace area of grants.gov provides some tools for managing multiple grants and required supplemental documents. In any case, now is the time to begin writing, organizing, and reviewing all required documents. Leave plenty of time to make deadlines. Notify the grants office that the proposal will arrive soon for internal review. Keep all other stakeholders updated. (See *Chapter 9* for more detail.)

Chapter 8 Glossary

- **Digital Object Identifier (DOI):** A unique alphanumeric string assigned by the publisher to identify a document, its contents, and its location on the Web (analogous to an ISBN number). Required in some types of grants for references.

- **Subject Matter Experts:** Individuals whose credentials, knowledge, and experience within a discipline qualify them as reliable resources for a particular project.

- **Grants Office/Officer:** Generically, the entity responsible for oversight and administration of the grant process at an institution. This may be a designated person, a function of the Development office, a faculty committee, or some other administrative structure.

8.1   Evidence Tells the Story

A strong proposal tells a compelling story, captures the imagination of reviewers through an innovative design, and aligns with a specific solicitation. A good narrative flow brings the proposed program to life. The funding agency also wants to know that your institution will support the project. Link the project to the mission of the college or university, which increases the likelihood of both agency and institutional support. Also ensure that the proposal is feasible, follows guidelines, and has impact, clarity, and durability. (See *Section 8.1.2* for details.)

In some cases, the project may have commercialization potential. Whatever the project's scope or ambition, a well thought out and clearly expressed narrative will help sway both the funding agency and end-users, investors, or other potential stakeholders. This may require paperwork and an independent evaluation by subject matter experts (SMEs). (See *Chapter 13* on small business grants for an overview.)

8.1.1 Make Your Case

The proposal narrative must be logical with reasoning that will convince the decision-makers to fund the program. Ensure that you create a balance between research summary and a realistic program design. Make certain the proposal follows all instructions from the solicitation.

Remember that a proposal's first audience is the team of reviewers who initially read and evaluate it. They can make or break your chances. Sometimes it is a federal review panel, sometimes a private family, sometimes an industry committee or corporate board that does the evaluation, but they are the first people the proposal must engage and convince. A best practice is to arrange proposal sections according to the solicitation, even if not required; this makes it more immediately understandable to the reviewers. In other words, make it easy for them to find all necessary components.

8.1.2 Style Requirements

Different types of writing have different styles (journal article, novel, textbook, etc.). The same can be said of proposal narratives. Develop a sense of what language and phrases work. Keep in mind that many who will read the narrative are not experts in the field. Even if they are, they may not have the same understanding of your subfield. Begin a repository of past proposals (accepted and rejected) that can be mined for phrases adaptable and reusable in new proposals.

The narrative should display style characteristics that directly engage the reviewers:

- **Impact:** Distinguish the submission from the crowd. Strike a balance between originality and overplay. A review panel can reject brilliant ideas, although novel and creative, because the concept promises unrealistic results or might be better suited for another program.

- **Clarity:** State the project's purpose sharply and directly. Proposals that leave any doubt or questions in the reviewers' minds reduce the chance of success. The narrative must substantiate a simply stated claim consistent with the overall intent of the grant program.

- **Durability:** Make the proposal framework compelling and memorable. Reviewers should be able to imagine the proposer as the one most likely to see the project successfully through to completion.

- **Feasibility:** Demonstrate that your organization's structure and resources fit the funding agency's guidelines. Does the institution or partner organizations have adequate resources or facilities to run the program? Are there well-articulated justification, significance, and/or impact statements?

The solicitation may include specific style instructions for the proposal, on everything: margins, font type and size, reference and citation formats, etc. It may ask for adherence to a particular style guide (Chicago, APA, IEEE, American Medical Association, etc.). If none is specified, just be consistent with the one you choose. Furthermore, since the first narrative paragraph should always contain the name of the institution, the title of the project, and the solicitation title, you may want to create a first-paragraph template adaptable to each project.

A Convincing Narrative

When making your case, support conclusions with solid evidence; asking for funding is a request rather than the more familiar academic scholarly article.

- **Necessary and Sufficient Conditions** A sound argument convinces because its supporting evidence (conditions) are both necessary and sufficient. A necessary condition must be part of the reasoning, but may not be enough on its own. Sufficient conditions are enough to make a sound argument and thus must include any necessary ones.

- **Logical Fallacies** Avoid logical fallacies at all cost. They damage an argument. There are several master lists of fallacies online; here is one of them:

  utminers.utep.edu/omwilliamson/engl1311/fallacies.htm

8.1.3   Merit Statements

Three common statements required in many proposals are Intellectual Merit, Broader Impact, and Broadening Participation. Even if these three are not explicitly required in the solicitation, it can be useful to include them; reviewers appreciate evidence of the context surrounding a focused idea. (See *Section 3.2* for examples and details.)

8.1.4   Literature Search

Do a literature search for proposals similar to yours before submission. Is your idea too close to another proposer's idea? You usually won't know about this going in (calculus, after all, was invented independently multiple times), but before submitting the proposal, check examples of previously funded or rejected proposals very carefully to help avoid this problem.

Searching for previously funded proposals is different from searching literature in your field. Consult with the credentialed librarians on campus for a more comprehensive search. They are trained in searching across multiple platforms for information that might otherwise escape you.

8.2   Include Supporting Documents

Required supporting documents vary depending on the funding agency and the solicitation. Some agencies are strict about which documents are permitted and how they are structured. Furthermore, limits are often placed on narrative length (usually 3 to 15 pages), font type size (usually

11 or 12 point), and margins, as well as other page layout parameters. Some files, such as the budget justification and data management plans, are discussed in detail elsewhere. (See *Section 7.2* and *9.6 for more*).

In partnerships, both home and partner institutions may have to supply their own corresponding documents. Note that each institution may need access to the funding agency's submission platform to upload their corresponding documents (e.g. the NSF), it is the home institution that is responsible for officially submitting the proposal.

Sometimes (often, for federal proposals) all of the pieces of the proposal must be submitted as separate files. As you prepare, it is a good idea to create a checklist of what is needed to fulfill the funding agency's guidelines. Some documents, such as the Facilities, Equipment, and other Resources statement, might become boilerplate forms that can be reused for other proposals. Table 8.1 shows a list of commonly requested documents with explanations. Most federal agencies require some or all of them.

Table 8.1: List of potential documents required by federal agencies.

Document	Explanation
Cover Sheet/Letter	An online form containing identification information.
Project Summary	One page that consists of a brief overview of the project, a broader impact statement, and an intellectual merit statement.

Continued on next page

Table 8.1 – continued from previous page

Document	Explanation
Table of Contents	If requested, a table of contents is usually generated automatically when the narrative is submitted by the funding agency software.
Project Narrative	It describes the project's scope and purpose, and explains how it will be executed.
References	The solicitation will dictate whether references should be a separate uploaded file or included at the end of the narrative. It is important to cross-check references. All should be cited in the narrative, and all cited sources should be listed in the references. It is also important that any references follow a consistent format.
Budget and Justification	A budget justification validates a project's expenses. (See *Chapter 7* for more details.) Funding agencies generally request aggregate sums (totals on salary, travel costs, materials, etc.); however, keeping a detailed spreadsheet for accurate dispersal of funds is important, too.
Current and Pending Grants/Proposals	This document lists all of the grantee's current grants and proposals under review.

Continued on next page

Table 8.1 – continued from previous page

Document	Explanation
Recent Collaborations	Some funding agencies require a list of all the people with whom senior personnel have recently collaborated, to avoid conflicts of interest when the proposal is under review.
Facilities, Equipment, and Other Resources	This is an aggregated description of the physical resources available for the project. The purpose of this statement is to demonstrate that there are sufficient facilities and equipment to successfully support and complete the project. This statement also includes informational resources, such as the library's research capacity, as well as the physical infrastructure.
Data Management Plan	This statement describes how data will be collected, handled, analyzed, chronicled, maintained, secured, and shared in the course of administering a project.
Mentoring Program, Post-doctoral Scholars	If postdocs are supported by the project, a description of mentoring activities is required.

Continued on next page

Table 8.1 – continued from previous page

Document	Explanation
Letter of Support	This letter is an official statement from the home institution describing its knowledge and support of the project. The letter should address how the project fits within the mission or strategic goals of the institution. It may address the PI's qualifications or ability to complete the project.
Letter of Collaboration[1]	This letter is an official statement indicating the signatory's intent to collaborate with the PI as described in the proposal (detailing responsibilities, materials, and availability of matching funds).
Letter of Commitment[1]	Similar to the collaboration letter, this letter indicates the signatory's intent to commit resources to the funded project, but not necessarily full collaboration. It may also give the signatory's rationale for supporting the project.
Curriculum Vitae (CV)	This is usually an abridged two-page version of each senior personnel's CV, containing only those elements relevant to the project.
Supplemental Materials	Additional relevant material providing evidence in support of the project's value (tables, presentations, video/audio files, etc.)

Please note some funding agencies may use different terms to identify similar supplemental elements related to those in Table 8.1. For instance, executive summaries or overview documents are similar to project summaries. All contain important project information. Likewise, information that is contained within the project narrative for a federal solicitation also may be requested as a separate document for other funding agencies (e.g., a description of the project team, key benefits, scope and limitations, impact on current projects, project success factors, an evaluation plan, a research plan).

8.3   Proposal Review

Reviewers at funding agencies initially rank the submitted proposals in order to identify the most promising ones. Some rely on internal staff and some choose external professionals for the initial review. For those funding agencies with external review panels, the panel provides input according to specific criteria aligned with the individual solicitation. The funding agency may have additional internal review processes, too, before decisions are made. Chosen reviewers have at least some advanced knowledge of the discipline, and can include government representatives, academics, and other subject matter experts. They must adhere to high professional standards and ethical behavior requirements.

In order to better understand a funding agency's process,

---

[1]Funding agencies will identify which letters are required with a proposal's submission.

one useful strategy is to sign on as a reviewer in your field, if the opportunity is available.

Although you cannot recreate this process in full (and it differs among agencies), it is helpful to mimic it before submission to correct errors and bolster evidence. (See *Subsection 8.3.1* and the practice box at the end of this chapter for a mock review process.)

8.3.1   Review Criteria

If you are interested in establishing a mock review process, here are some suggested criteria. In our experience, these four considerations are central to every review process, but you may want to add more questions or criteria.

Criterion 1: Administrative review and overview

Submitting a proposal that is incomplete, missing even one small piece, is enough for the funding agency to reject the proposal application. Attention to detail is crucial.

1. Does the proposal have all the parts requested in the solicitation?

2. Does the proposal make clear which of the program priorities would be addressed?

3. Are the required components and supplemental documents submitted in the proper order and format?

Criterion 2: Significance and alignment

The strongest proposals mirror the goals, intent, and context of the solicitation. Significant proposals will have the potential to extend the funding impact beyond its original intent.

1. How significant/important is the proposed project?

2. Would it advance the missions, goals, or priorities of both the related agency and the proposing college or university? Be specific.

3. Does the project impact stakeholders beyond the immediate audience of the funding agency and/or institution? Be specific.

Criterion 3: Approach

Funding agencies assess proposals based on the likelihood of success, project design, management, and available resources. Clarity is key.

1. Does the proposal address potential pitfalls/problems or alternative approaches?

2. Does the proposal clearly communicate program structure?

3. Does the proposal offer honest evaluation of friction points or other potential difficulties? Does it outline solutions?

Criterion 4: Merit Review Criteria

Even if the solicitation does not explicitly call for them, it is a good idea to include language supporting at least one of the following: Intellectual Merit, Broader Impact, or Broadening Participation. (See *Section 3.2* for details.)

1. Intellectual Merit: Does the proposal have the potential to advance knowledge in the field?

2. Broader Impact: Does the proposal encompass the potential to benefit society, per the solicitation?

3. Broadening Participation: Does the proposal help build a diverse and capable workforce?

8.4   Proposal Submission

Funding agencies often have specific submission instructions, protocols, and deadlines. Failure to adhere to these rules will disqualify a submission. Much of the time, the PI works with a grants officer, who reviews it for completeness before submitting it on behalf of the PI and the institution. This is particularly true for federal grants, but also other types of agencies and foundations.

The agency may reject proposals that do not follow exact specifications. Before submission, ensure that the institution supports the grant request, that the proposal has been through all the appropriate channels, that it meets all the requirements of the solicitation, and that it includes all the supporting documents.

Therefore:

- Follow all the pre-submission requirements. Register to submit, if needed. NSF, for example, requires that your grants officer signs off on your application for an account, to confirm your identity. On the other hand, private foundations may hire outside companies to vet your credentials.

- Check and recheck your proposal and all supporting material for mistakes (grammar, page limits, references, citations, layout, etc.).

- Submit through the appropriate administrative office (usually the grants office, but it could be development or another assigned department). Some agencies will allow you to upload the relevant documents before submission. Others will require the grants officer to both upload and submit. Verify that you have included all the required documents.

- Many funding agencies and solicitations have hard deadlines; some do not. There may be a requirement at your institution to submit the finished proposal to a grants office for review. It is good practice to create an internal finish deadline ahead of the actual deadline in order to leave enough time for any institutional reviews.

- Do not submit the same proposal to more than one agency at the same time, i.e. "double dipping." This is an issue for federal and some private sources. Quoting your own research, i.e. "self-plagiarism," also may be an issue. Funding agencies provide guidance and rules, but if you have questions, contact the program officer.

Wait time for approval can vary widely. While waiting, think up new ideas, collaborate with others, and prepare for approval. (See *Chapter 9* for more.) If your proposal succeeds, see *Chapter 10* on administering the grant. If your proposal is declined, see *Chapter 11* for analysis of rejected proposals.

Do not be discouraged if your proposal is unsuccessful; many first attempts are declined. Reflect on feedback (if provided), talk with others, generate new ideas, and most important: think about resubmission, even if you have to change your approach. Do a cost/benefit analysis—is it worth it to revise and resubmit to the same solicitation or a different one? Even if you start over, there is likely to be boilerplate material from the original (facilities statement, for example) that will be useful in the next proposal.

PRACTICE THIS: A Mock Review

Once your team finishes a draft, find time to conduct a mock review. Develop a list of review criteria, beginning with the four in *Section 8.3.1*. You may wish to add more criteria or questions. Agency scoring systems differ somewhat, and solicitations vary in their requirements, but this is the general process:

1. Assemble a trusted team of mock reviewers who have knowledge of the general subject area, but were not involved in writing the proposal. People with fresh eyes will be better equipped to see gaps.

2. Allow sufficient time before the meeting for your team to do a close read and evaluation, using your list of review criteria.

3. Schedule a time when the team can meet, discuss, and score the proposal. Alternatively, the comments and scoring could be submitted electronically to the PI.

Reviewers should score each criterion according to the grading scheme below, accompanying each choice with explanatory sentences that note gaps or inconsistencies. It is especially important to discuss the low scores.

- 3 = excellent to exceptional
- 2 = satisfactory to very good
- 1 = poor to fair

Tally an average score for each criterion. If any average is less than 3, take a look at those parts of the proposal and make improvements.

Chapter 9

Set Up for Success

Set up needed campus structures

A critical part of proposal development is to anticipate success as you prepare it, no matter the length. If you get positive news from a funding agency only to find out you need to start immediately and still need significant details worked out, successful grant administration becomes more difficult. These tasks often require problem-solving and patience, so get started early. Pre-planning can be time-consuming, but the good news is that once created, needed structures can be reused for the next grant with only minor edits. (See *Chapter 7* for planning a budget, *Chapter 10* for finalizing arrangements, and *Chapter 12* for building them into a grant culture.)

Glossary

- **Algorithm:** A process or procedure to be followed as part of a problem-solving approach when searching for solutions.

- **Metadata:** A collection of data that describes and summarizes information about other data.

- **Confidential Data:** Personal identifiable information that should not be obtained or disclosed without permission.

- **Taxpayer Identification Number (TIN):** an umbrella term that comprises several different types of tax IDs, including social security number (SSN) and employer identification number (EIN).

- **Informational Infrastructure:** Encompasses the intellectual resources available within an institution to support scholarly endeavors.

- **Resources vs. Facilities vs. Equipment:** The descriptions of these three often overlap. When developing a proposal it is often useful to make distinctions among them. In this text, "facilities" refers to infrastructure, "equipment" refers to instrumentation and hardware, and "resources" refers to any other assets that can be drawn on to successfully implement the project.

9.1 When to plan?

In effective grantsmanship, there is a fine balance between planning and administration. Sometimes preparation has to wait until the project starts (the final schedule for participant orientation, for example); however, certain elements can be anticipated and should be prepared for while still writing the proposal. As an example, suppose your proposal requires on-campus housing and meals for participants. Contacting housing and food services ahead of time is necessary to learn availability, costs, and location. This gives you time to make other arrangements or adjust your proposal if some of these are not available.

Grant administration requires good time management: the time to run the program itself (organize events, communicate with participants, schedule facilities, etc.) plus the time to keep track of data needed for an accurate and comprehensive report. Various administrative functions can be set up early to streamline processes. Discuss and confirm with your department chair, relevant administrators, and all needed service departments how their contributions to the grant will work, what resources it will require, and particularly how the PI and senior personnel will discharge teaching and committee responsibilities at the same time. Document those conversations. Note that some grants may not involve as many campus entities; however, it is still important to think everything through ahead of time. This chapter and the next will go over both preparing and administering separate elements of the grant processes in detail.

Your time is limited. Make sure you have arranged your

schedule to meet professional obligations while administering the grant. Negotiating release time and other support ensures that the administration values your efforts.

9.2   Initial Department Discussions

Even before starting to write the proposal, take time to discuss teaching schedules and related issues with the department chair. Scheduling can make a real difference to the successful execution of the project; if there is no way to reduce the total number of classes, can they at least offer fewer preps, or arrange to have most classes on fewer days? Some grants (not all) allow the budget to include funds for administrative assistance or an adjunct hire to lower teaching load. Additionally, ask if working on the proposal or administering the grant can be considered service or professional development (i.e., is grant work equivalent to faculty committee membership?). Finally, negotiate for space and resources needed to execute the project.

9.3   Service Office Discussions

Staff are most knowledgeable about their offices' services, but their experience is often underutilized. Thus it is in the PI's best interest to consult them in advance. This could involve when to schedule access to shared equipment, required oversight, and needed resources such as dining, security, housing, meeting spaces, IT, audio-visual, etc. They may not be able to formally schedule or block out time in advance, but let them know a possibility exists and you may approach them later for their advice. If you need a website or document database (federal grants often require public dissemination) sketch out a design for that now and identify a developer on campus if necessary.

9.3.1 Vendor Registration

Many institutions now require that a company be registered as a vendor before business can be conducted with that company. If your institution has such a requirement, and the project needs services, facility usage, or materials from an unregistered vendor, ask the company to register in advance so they are able to do business when the time comes.

9.3.2 Library Services

Some grants may require library services. For example, off-campus participants may need library access to conduct project activities. Early conversations with the library help facilitate grant success.

9.4 Administration Discussions

Keep the upper administration informed of any agreements and plans. Have a conversation with the IRB committee (see *Section 6.3*), and make certain you know what status you require (you may be exempt from regulations, and you may also need to explain that to the IRB in detail, particularly if the grant hosts people from outside the institution who are participants and not human subjects).

Prepare formative and summative assessment documents, such as surveys, focus group questionnaires, etc., that may be needed, and submit them for approval if required by the IRB or another evaluative body.

9.5   Internal Official Documents

Many projects will utilize required documents (e.g., invitation letters, photo release and other permission forms, and visa considerations). These must conform to institutional criteria and include official language. What is needed will vary widely, of course, depending on the nature of the grant and the requirements of the institution. Ask Human Resources for their templates as a starting point; these may need editing to match project goals and objectives. Human Resources or Institutional Counsel should approve any adjustments. If templates do not exist, work with those departments to develop them.

9.5.1   Documents to Prepare in Advance

No matter the type of grant, there are most likely numerous documents and forms to be completed by the PI, senior personnel, and any participants. Contacting HR, Accounts Payable, and other campus offices in advance helps with having documents prepared and ready to go well before the start of the program.

- Tax Forms: If the project involves paying participants, government tax forms will be required. HR requests these forms be completed before the program starts.

- W-4 Federal tax form to be filled out by any senior personnel or participant for whom taxes are being withheld (if they are not already on the institution's payroll).

- W-9 Federal tax form to be filled out by any senior personnel or participant for whom taxes are not being withheld (stipends, honoraria, etc.). This provides the correct Taxpayer Identification Number (TIN) to the employer.

- I-9 Form: Verifies the identity and employment authorization of an individual.

- State Tax Withholding Form: Similar to a federal W-4 form, for state income tax withholding.

• Release and Permission Forms: These forms are often mandated by state or federal governments. Therefore they may be required of all participants, but are essential when working with younger students who need parental permission.

• Summative and Formative Assessments: These include surveys, questionnaires, and other forms of program evaluation. They must undergo IRB approval before implementation.

• Background Checks: Required of all senior personnel and mentors in programs involving minors.

• Invitation letters: Sent to potential participants (speakers, attendees, students, etc.). These may require editing and approval by the administration.

- Other Forms: There may be additional forms for items such as housing, reimbursement, instructions on appropriate behavior, and special needs or meal restrictions, among others.

9.6   Data Management Plans

Data management plans play a critical role in proposal evaluation. During the merit review, evaluators consider:

- A description of the materials to be produced over the course of the project—types of data, samples, curriculum materials, metadata, etc. This also includes describing the standards used for collecting and storing data, what file formats will be used, and how the information will be archived.

- Accountability—what are the roles and responsibilities of all parties with respect to data management? What are the contingency plans if key personnel leave the project?

- How will data be shared? What policies will be in place for public access and re-use of the data?

- Where appropriate, what actions will be taken to ensure privacy, confidentiality, and security of subjects involved in the project? How will intellectual property rights be protected?

9.6.1   Data Management for Reports

All grants require a final report, and many will also require periodic reports. Although the specific components may differ, base the data collection and management system on the funding agency's required information categories. As a best practice, keep track of more than you will need, and ensure that it is easy to update as you go. A sample report form appears in *Section 10.4*. NSF provides a reporting template usable as a general guide; other agencies may or may not provide a template.

In short: keep track of everything, duplicate all records, keep more information than you think you will need, assign backup for all roles (redundancy), and insist on accountability from collaborators.

9.6.2   Data Management for Dissemination

Investigators are often expected to share data, samples, and other supporting materials produced as a result of work on the project. In fact, federal agencies require a data management plan as part of the proposal that describes how the investigator will follow an agency's policy on disseminating and sharing research results, subject to confidentiality restrictions. Many funding agencies and foundations require public dissemination of materials, results, and products developed by the funded project. Institutional and agency policies will guide your efforts to secure, store, and/or disseminate project material, including policies on how to create and post a web page on the institution's server.

Unless subject to confidentiality restrictions, most data management statements usually include plans for dissemination of two types: internal and external. It is important to keep your organization apprised of appropriate project results and accomplishments (internal dissemination). It is also necessary to describe how you will secure and/or share results outside your organization (external dissemination).

Dissemination could be as simple as posting progress on a website set up specifically for the project, or it may require setting up a public repository for storing various kinds of data—algorithms, metadata, videos, peer-reviewed publications, special-issue conference proceedings, presentations, classroom modules—basically any professional material that can be traced to the project.

Coordinate with the IT office to design and post a web page that contains information about the project, as well as how updates will be added as the project proceeds. The IT office will also need to be involved if a repository is to hold data and products developed as a result of the project, and will need to provide multiple types of security based on the type of data. Some funding agencies may require public access to such repositories. If not, some thought will have to be given to who will have access and how someone will gain access.

9.7   Contingency Planning

Even the best planning is subject to Murphy's Law. Things rarely go exactly according to the original plan, but there is always a solution. There is no need to stress about it. Remember that funding agencies frequently encounter unforeseen problems and can often help. Some issues experienced by the authors and their solutions appear below; there are of course many more.

- **Example 1:** Some grants require external evaluators. In this example, the evaluator had to exit the project at the last minute because of a family emergency. The PI needed to find a replacement quickly.

  Possible Solutions: First ask the outgoing evaluator for a recommendation, or ask other people who have used different evaluators for a reference. Since the outgoing evaluator's plan is in the proposal, you can explain to the funding agency that you will implement the plan while you seek a new evaluator.

- **Example 2:** In planning the culmination of the grant project, the PI reserved a multi-use auditorium, including the stage, for a week-long conference. Subsequently the Theater Department scheduled its spring performance during the same week. Since the scheduling software showed no time conflict, the facilities office scheduled the performance and saw no reason to notify the PI. However, they did not take into account that during the week of a performance, the play's stage set remained in place. This presented a problem because the speakers could not use the stage.

  Possible Solutions: Via mutual discussion, the theater manager, play director, and the PI reached an accord. The theater moved some of the stage set back after each performance to allow the curtains to close and the AV screen to be used during the day. The PI agreed to place the podium on the auditorium floor.

- **Example 3:** The authors experienced several situations in which budgetary needs changed over the life of a grant, or even between proposal submission and grant award. In one example, the proposal budget included funds to purchase expensive hardware in order to complete the project. However in the months between submission and award, the technology advanced to the point where the hardware was obsolete and replaced with far less expensive, and more powerful, software. That resulted in a large surplus of funds specifically designated for hardware; consequently the grant could not be spent out.

  Possible Solutions: One possibility is to refund the surplus money, but this creates issues for the funding agencies, and may impact the success of future proposal submissions, so this "solution" should be avoided. A better approach would be to contact the funding agency and discuss the possibility of amending the grant with an addendum for alternative use of the funding.

PRACTICE THIS: What if plans go awry?

Review the chapter, and select three of the planning elements. For example, one planning element could be negotiating with the department chair and administration for use of space or release time.

1. Draft a plan for the three elements you selected.

2. Think about what could go wrong with each of the elements.

3. Brainstorm some solutions for each of the elements.

Chapter 10

Administer the Grant

Chapter 10 Glossary

- **Orientation:** A formally organized event at the out-set of a project that introduces participants to processes, procedures, and responsibilities.

- **Letters of Invitation:** Sent to potential participants (speakers, attendees, students, etc.). These may require editing and approval by the administration.

- **Release Forms:** These forms are often mandated by state or federal governments; therefore, they may be required of all participants, but are essential when working with younger students who need parental permission.

- **Dissemination:** The circulation and publication of information, data, and products of the program (journal articles, algorithms, modules, etc.). This is often required by the funding agency within a specific time-frame.

10.1   Notify and Communicate

While waiting for final approval, prepare documents, finalize an orientation program, fine-tune your data collection process, review dissemination and reporting procedures (including web design), and inform senior personnel, partners, and on-campus service departments.

As soon as formal approval arrives, tell your department chair and the grant office or committee, contact the communications office for an official announcement, and get your team together to celebrate. (Remember to document these communications.) Then get started. Do as much as possible in advance of the funding start date. Try to anticipate any issues that might arise.

Sometimes there will be a gap of a month or two between when the award is announced and the money is actually available, which is preferable because it allows time to finalize arrangements, contact participants, order supplies, and so on. Other times you might have only a week or two.

The structure of a project determines a grant's administrative complexity. Unfortunately, all types of grants can be equally time-consuming. For example, a grant supporting the faculty member's research generally has fewer moving parts than a grant with multiple strategies or external partnerships. However, there are always pertinent details (lab protocols, IRB requirements, various costs, other planning elements) that need substantial PI attention. Managing these details takes time, and should be taken seriously.

Here's where pre-planning smooths the path forward; you will have already thought through who to call, what to request, and what start-up tasks need to be done in what order.

Among the initial tasks:

- Coordinate with the Public Relations office to draft a statement so it is ready for release once final approval arrives for the project.

- Contact each of the needed service departments in

writing and finalize scheduling. This might include requesting shared equipment, dining/catering facilities, meeting rooms, security, housing, IT, audio-visual, and/or website final design and implementation.

- Set up meetings with senior personnel, the grants office, department chair, staff, accounts payable, and any other involved people/offices. Clear up any problems and misunderstandings; make certain everyone knows what to do and when. If an expected resource has evaporated, get help finding an alternative. (See *Section 9.7 for contingency planning.*)

- Complete any administrative paperwork. If you will be inviting participants (for a conference, for example), send out the invitations.

- Collect participant forms (W9, payroll, release, background checks, etc.) from HR and other offices. Note that some of these forms will have to be submitted well in advance. (See *Section 9.5.1* for a more complete list of these.)

- Recognize that many months pass between submission and award. Notify the funding agency of any significant change in personnel, partners, or location. The project design cannot be changed.

10.2   Orientation

Projects with multiple participants greatly benefit from a well-planned orientation. Different groups on and off campus may need to be included in it: partners, student helpers, administrative staff, officials, senior personnel, etc. If the grant supports professional meetings and other group activities, an orientation informs participants of project expectations, procedures, and criteria.

Depending on the participants' experience and background, the orientation for these types of activities could include people introducing themselves to each other, a presentation about ethical research behavior (if anyone is new to research), an outline of goals and objectives, a discussion of activities to be supported by the project, and an overview of what constitutes appropriate costs as well as how participants are to be reimbursed. Distribute the finalized agenda to all stakeholders prior to the orientation.

A Sample Orientation Schedule

An NSF Research Experiences for Undergraduates (REU) program is a good example of a grant that benefits from a robust orientation. Hundreds of REUs across the country engage students in meaningful research projects for eight to ten weeks, mostly in the summer, away from their home institutions, to introduce them to STEM careers. Both participants and mentors benefit from an initial orientation because it clarifies expectations and responsibilities. See *Table 10.1* for an example of an orientation program.

Table 10.1: Sample orientation for an REU program

Time	Description
09:00 - 09:45	**Campus Tour**
09:45 - 12:00	**Breakfast**
10:00 - 10:30	**Welcome and Introductions** • Mentors and staff introduce themselves to participants. • Participants introduce themselves to each other.
10:30 - 11:00	**Program Information** • Program overview • Participant responsibilities • Resources and FAQ • Administrative forms
11:00 - 11:30	**Equipment and Software** • Overview of available software and equipment and software used for research during the program.
11:30 - 12:30	**Ethics in Research Workshop** • Breakout sessions: discuss case studies. • Return to discuss as a group.
12:30 - 13:30	**Lunch**
13:30 - 14:00	**Focus Group** • Expectations for theof a research program. • Future education goals.
14:00 - 16:00	**Meet with Mentors**

10.3 Expenditures

Grants require spending out the funds appropriately and within the allotted time, while abiding by guidelines from both the institution and the funding agency. This is important. Remember, because funding agencies are required to distribute a certain amount, returning unspent funds presents them with difficulties. (See *Section 7.3.2* for more detail.)

There are several main ways to pay for services, purchases, and personnel. Each comes with its own issues and benefits. Some institutions will issue the PI a credit card for grant expenditures, which makes paying grant expenses easier and quicker, but means the PI is directly responsible for the use and security of the card, keeping receipts, and checking them against the billing statement. Using a reimbursement process avoids the pitfalls (such as loss) of a credit card, but it also means a delay in reimbursement for costs paid out of pocket, and there is still some record-keeping paperwork. You will need to decide what works best.

Solicitation and institutional policies set the parameters for grant expenditures: costs must be allowable, reasonable, necessary, allocable, and consistent with those policies. Explanation alone does not make a cost allowable; there must be language in both the solicitation and institutional policy that permits the expense. (See *Section 7.3* for a full description and worked out examples of these terms.) In addition to being allowable, costs must also be reasonable and necessary, showing good judgment on price comparison, vendor choice, and responsibility to the institution. Finally, the costs must be demonstrably beneficial to the grant program's success (i.e., allocable).

10.3.1   Expenditure Records

Maintaining accurate and complete financial records of what has been spent is critical to the successful administration of a grant and helps keep the door open for future grants. An audit is a real possibility under any circumstances, and having good, accurate records will not only ensure a smooth one, but will also help secure future grant opportunities.

10.3.2   Additional Considerations

Different institutions have different expenditure procedures and regulations. Discuss with the institution's financial offices the best way to proceed.

- Keep track of your own expenditures even if the accounting office or online software is also doing it.

- Although rare, funding agencies may conduct an audit of grant expenditures. Accurate and complete records will help ensure a smooth process. Keep records up to date continuously.

- Check how much money is left in the grant frequently; this is as important as knowing what has been spent so you can gauge whether you are spending money in the allotted time.

- If there are participants on the grant, you can choose to pay their expenses directly (booking travel, housing, planning meals, etc.) Alternatively, you can reimburse allowable participant expenses as they occur. In both cases, there are advantages and disadvantages.

- – Paying participant expenses directly ensures that the expenses are within allowable and reasonable parameters, but requires more logistics on the part of the PI.

- – Reimbursing participant expenses shifts logistics to the participant, but the PI must now monitor, review, and either approve or reject the expenditures.

- Direct payment to vendors may require the PI to coordinate and seek approval from the institution. Some institutions insist on a bid process, or require vendors be registered before doing business with them.

10.4   Reporting

Regular reporting to the funding agency on project progress is an important component of grant administration, yet often neglected until late in the reporting period. Ongoing programs require monitoring, assessing, and adjustments as they progress, and continual assessment places the program on a positive trajectory. Private foundations are often less structured than government agencies. Reports to federal agencies are more elaborate, but they generally provide templates. Any report will contain a subset of the data you are gathering; there will be much more detail to capture, presumably on a spreadsheet. Write down minutiae even if you think it may not be needed in the report.

Note that some grant offices assist in writing and submitting reports. However, the PI feeds that process, and must know the jargon and items the funding agency requires. A word of caution: the PI is the one held accountable for the content and timely submission of all reports.

Keep records of everything, beginning when the preliminary announcement happens; this makes it much easier to write and file the required reports. Keeping up-to-date and complete records will save many headaches down the road. If you developed an efficient data-gathering system while you wrote the proposal, you are way ahead. Get into the habit of recording essential information while the events are still fresh in your memory; this makes reporting much easier. (See *Section 9.6.1* for planning work.)

Keep in mind, reporting involves more than records of expenditures and results. You will also want to address the experience of participants by following up regularly with them to find out what they are getting out of the program. If you are working with students, you may need to follow up with them some years later. Ask them for backup contact information, particularly if their student contact information will change when they graduate.

10.4.1   Sample Report Entries

Reporting structure varies among funding agencies. Reporting allows transparency on how the funds are being used, aids stakeholders' understanding of the grant's impact, and assists in accountability for the use of grant funds. Below is a selection of questions—in no particular order and not comprehensive—the answers to which might be required in a report.

- What was accomplished? What was learned?

- What were the major goals of the project?

- What was accomplished under these goals? Provide information for at least one of the four categories below:

  - Major activities

  - Specific objectives

  - Significant results

  - Key outcomes and other achievements

- What opportunities for training and professional development has the project provided?

- How have the results been disseminated to relevant audiences?

- What do you plan to do during the next reporting period to accomplish the goals?

- What are products generated by the project? (These might be some of the following: publications, technologies or techniques, inventions, patent applications, licenses, websites, databases, physical collections, audio/video products, software, models, educational aids, curricula, instruments, equipment, video tutorials, or supporting files.)

- What participants and other collaborating organizations have worked on or been involved in the project?

- What are the impacts of the project? How have they contributed? Consider impacts on the following:

  - Development of the principle discipline(s) of the project

  - Other disciplines

  - The development of human resources

  - Institutional and non-institutional resources that build or maintain infrastructure (physical, informational, structural) (See *Section 8.3.1* for more.)

  - Technology transfer

  - Society in general

- Were there problems in approach or other reasons for subsequent changes?

  - Actual or anticipated problems, or delays and actions, or plans to resolve them

  - Changes that have significant impact on expenditures

  - Significant changes in use or care of human subjects or animals

  - Significant changes in the handling of biohazards

10.5 Dissemination

Dissemination is important for all stakeholders involved in the project, from the PI to the participants to the institution to the funding agency. It promotes all three types of merit criteria, enhances project visibility and sustainability, and draws attention to its successes. Review *Section 9.6.2* for planning work.

A public record of project accomplishments professionally benefits everyone involved. Furthermore, if the project exceeds grant expectations, it improves the funding agency's credentials. This has the effect of raising your profile at that agency and establishing your reputation as a successful grant administrator, which contributes to building a robust grant culture at your institution and facilitates productive partnerships.

10.5.1 Types of Dissemination

Dissemination comes in many forms and depends on the type of project.

- A regularly updated website is a primary instance of dissemination, and can serve as a program hub and an information repository. It centralizes all the activities in one place, and encourages others to build on them.

- If the project involves organizing events (conferences, workshops, meetings, etc.), publishing a post-event synopsis establishes a summative record of what took place.

- Many funded projects lead to scholarly products such as conference proceedings, peer-reviewed publications, modules, courses, curricula, or visual and performing arts, which can be linked on the project website.

- Other products could include additional educational materials, audio and video presentations, algorithms, software, models, and equipment, among others.

10.5.2   Repository Security and Access

As noted above, information repositories are essential for dissemination. Any repository will likely have different levels of security because there exist conflicting goals and responsibilities with regard to such information. It is essential to identify what can be shared, how to disseminate it, and to whom. The PI must make these distinctions within federal and institutional regulations.

Examples of freely shared information include conference proceedings, journal publications, educational materials, artworks, or performances.

Examples of restricted access information include raw data from medical or psychological research (protecting human subject confidentiality), projects involving minors, endangered species, or military research.

Additional notes:

- Again, have procedures in place for dissemination with the appropriate offices even before the grant is awarded. (See *Chapter 9* on planning.)

- Remember that professional journals have specific formatting requirements for publishing or archiving data; professional societies often provide guidance on how to disseminate information within that community.

- Organizations, funding agencies, university libraries, and repository registries offer resources and training on dissemination and data management best practices.

PRACTICE THIS: Planning and Execution

1. Pick out three administrative elements and develop a strategy for successfully implementing them at your institution.

2. Pick three kinds of information that your project will generate. Develop a dissemination plan for all three.

Chapter 11

Analyzing a Rejection

Receiving Disappointing News

Sooner or later, every grant writer gets disappointing news about a proposal. This might happen less often as the writer's experience grows, but there will always be some rejections. Rather than give up, analyze why the proposal was not funded and turn it into a learning experience. Remember that you can't control some realities: inexperienced reviewers, hidden agendas, the content of competing proposals, and the limited number of awards the granting organization can make based on a fixed budget. For the things you can address, however, start with an After-Action Review (AAR).

Chapter 11 Glossary

- **Digital Object Identifier (DOI):** A unique alphanumeric string assigned by the publisher to identify a document, its contents, and its location on the Web (analogous to an ISBN number).

- **After Action Review (AAR):** Term adapted from its original use in the military as a debriefing analysis of a project's strengths and weaknesses: what took place, why it happened, and how to improve on it.

- **Review Panel:** A group of reviewers invited by the funding agency to evaluate proposals. Reviewers are generally chosen based on their knowledge of the subject matter. The final decision rests with the funding agency.

11.1   The After Action Review

An AAR begins with analyzing reviewer comments, if available. You can also learn from your own analysis, and from your network of collaborators, mentors, and trainees past and present. Initiate your AAR with these questions.

- **Did you read the reviewers' comments (if provided) critically?** Do not take a rejected proposal personally. Even if some comments appear unhelpful, some will be actionable for this or future proposals. It's best to incorporate the constructively critical points into the next proposal as much as possible—especially if you have the opportunity to resubmit.

- **Did the proposal observe all of the solicitation's layout requirements?** This can get really picky: fonts, headings, margins, reference format, and length, among others. The NSF, for example, will mark down or summarily reject a proposal that has embedded links, references that are not cited in the narrative, incorrect supplemental documents, or even slightly smaller margins to make the narrative shorter. In contrast, many NIH agencies require embedded links for reference DOI (digital object identifier) numbers. Funding agencies all have different formatting rules, so your AAR should evaluate whether the proposal followed those unique rules. Federal and other funding agencies may take proposals through a preliminary review before they are sent to review panels, and if the proposal fails that, it will not be considered or scored for content review.

- **Did the proposal contain typos or grammatical errors?** "Small" mistakes such as referring to Figure 3 when you meant Figure 2 can lead to reviewer confusion about the message, suggest a lack of attention to detail, or result in tougher scrutiny or unfavorable comparison with other proposals under consideration.

- **Did the proposal have all required sections in the order listed in the solicitation?** It is a good idea to lay out the structure of the whole proposal before you begin to write, putting headings in the same order as they appear in the solicitation. This may not be required, but it is easier for the reviewer to read and evaluate.

- **Is the request sufficiently, but not excessively, innovative?** This is a tough one, since you will not know entirely what parameters the reviewers are using. Funding agencies often deny requests for additional funding for a currently supported project. On the other hand, reviewers may reject a project so unusual that the connection to the discipline appears unclear, and thus they conclude it lacks feasibility.

- **Has someone with fresh eyes (and preferably grant experience) read and commented on the proposal?** While it is best to have an internal proposal review before it is submitted—see *Section 8.3* for instructions—outside readers can be helpful with a rejected proposal. Additionally, you can apply to become a reviewer at a funding agency, if such a position is available, in order to gain perspective.

- **Was the idea too close to another proposer's idea?** You usually won't know about this going in, but before resubmitting the proposal, check again for examples of previously funded projects to help avoid this problem.

- **Did the proposal detail the team's ability to carry out the actions in the grant request using available facilities and resources?** Reviewers pay particular attention to this question. For example, is there sufficient expertise among the senior personnel to successfully address the issues outlined in the proposal? Are labs or rooms available to accommodate participants?

- **Did the proposal budget ask for equipment that could be obtained through other means?** For example, if you request a quadrupole time-of-flight liquid chromatograph-mass spectrometer for some portion of the work and have inconvenient, but adequate, access to the instrument at another institution, a review panel might question the need for funding unless the proposal clearly explains why the current situation is untenable.

- **Did the proposal clearly describe Intellectual Merit, Broadening Participation, and Broader Impact (if one or more of those sections are in the solicitation)?** The importance of the merit criteria was fully addressed in *Section 3.2*, and is reviewed below because of its significance for success.

  Intellectual Merit answers the question, "How does this project contribute to and advance the relevant body or bodies of knowledge?"

  Broader Impact answers "How might this project potentially benefit society as a whole, in ways not directly addressed in the grant?"

  Broadening Participation answers "How does this project contribute specifically to building a diverse and capable workforce vital to maintaining the nation's standard of excellence?"

- **Does your budget match the budget justification and goals outlined in the proposal?** Have you ensured that the budget aligns with the budget justification? For example, have you clearly justified personnel responsibilities to warrant their inclusion in the proposal? Some agencies limit how much personnel time can be covered in the budget; know the limits and stay within them.

11.2   Adjust, Rewrite, Resubmit

There is no need to throw out a rejected proposal and start over from scratch; pieces of it will be useful as boilerplate or as a springboard to other proposals.

Most proposals to federal agencies are internally triaged to determine whether they should be assigned to a review panel. If your proposal is peer reviewed, you will receive reviewer comments to guide future improvements. A few comments may give the impression the reviewer could have read the proposal more closely, but most comments will be useful indicators for how to strengthen future proposals. Sometimes a review panel may suggest that a rejected proposal be revised and then re-submitted. Some funding agencies provide details on the number of times a particular proposal may be resubmitted and what revisions are required. You can always contact the program officer to ask questions. In any case, experience leads to greater success.

Some editorial suggestions to strengthen or clarify a narrative appear below.

- **Change passive voice to active voice.**
  Example: *"The participants will complete the lab work,"* instead of "The lab work will be completed by the participants."

- **Avoid repeating the same structure or words.**
  "After collecting the data, I will conduct the analysis,
  instead of "I will collect the data and I will conduct
  the analysis."

- **Avoid strings of prepositional phrases.**
  *"Before I organize the agenda for the conference, I will
  write the participants' letters of invitation,"* instead of
  "While I write the letters of invitation for the participants, I will organize the agenda for the conference."

- **Avoid wordiness and unnecessary information.**
  *"In spite of limited housing options, the Center's acous-
  tics make it the best location for the conference,"* instead of "In spite of the fact that the Center is having
  difficulty finding appropriate housing for speakers, the
  conference will still be held at the facility because it
  has the best acoustics."

- **Experiment with strategies that deal with page
  limitations.**
  Conforming to page limitations for a narrative is tricky.
  One that exceeds guidelines will be summarily rejected.
  Reviewers will also reject text that has been artifi-
  cially padded. In addition to these suggestions, there
  are useful editorial strategies. It is usually easier to
  condense narrative than to expand it. For example,
  shorten paragraphs to remove an orphan (one word
  on a single line), often by choosing a shorter synonym
  for a longer word earlier in the paragraph. (For additional professional editing tips see *Appendix C.*)

Some projects will be difficult (but not impossible) to fund with a federal grant. Alternatively, private foundations—which have different guidelines—are worth a look when re-tooling a proposal for resubmission.

PRACTICE THIS: Interpreting Comments

Review panel comments can often be helpful, but other times confusing or irrelevant. The list below consists of a few possibilities. Describe which ones seem to be valuable critiques (worthwhile to improve a future proposal) and which ones seem off-course.

- "The authors spent a lot of time/space explaining or describing the project ideas, but were not explicit how those ideas would be implemented at the participant level."

- "I struggled to understand the roles of the multiple stakeholders and how they will benefit from their participation in the project. What expertise do they have? How will they apply their expertise to the project?"

- One particular solicitation emphasized supporting alternative forms of informal education outside of a standard school setting. Interpret the following comment from a review panel member: "Why is it necessary to provide professional development to alternative instructors? Why not bring experienced school teachers to this program instead?"

- "This project concentrates on the impact of citizen science to climate change, but the activities are place-based. How are place-based activities related to climate change?"

- "The proposal read like a research paper. Relevant clarifying details were missing about implementation and thus ability to successfully carry out the project goals."

Chapter 12

Building on Success

Provost Dr. Smith arrived at her new college to find that a grant had purchased an advanced 3D printer for interdisciplinary uses, but it was seldom used. Smith knew that 3D printing and scanning were important skill sets in multiple areas, so she hired an adjunct to teach a course in it, open to any student, and then invited speakers to talk about how the technology impacted several professions. She then obtained a small grant to organize a full day conference on the technology, open to the community and business leaders. Regional partners joined the college for a larger proposal to the state government and won a $250,000 award. This funded a center housing the latest in 3D technologies, open to both the college and community.

Chapter 12 Glossary

- **Grant culture**: A cornerstone of institutions in which grant development is fully networked, supported, and encouraged, resulting in a sustainable flow of funds to aid the entire fundraising effort.

- **Ideation:** The process of formulating, discovering, discussing, and conceptualizing project ideas and then matching one or more of them to appropriate funding solicitations. (See *Chapter 3* for details.)

12.1   Individual Faculty Mentoring

Previous chapters have outlined how to develop a good idea, mold it into a fundable project, and construct a strong proposal. The next step is to begin building an institutional network of grant-seeking faculty and to share that knowledge. This is the core of a mature grant culture.

There are three complementary features of grant culture: encouraging knowledge-sharing, establishing guidance and support, and creating institutional incentives. This book delineates the three separately to present a clearer picture of how they interlock, although they often grow simultaneously rather than in sequence. Another way to visualize a grant culture is through a flywheel of sustainable actions. (See *Figure 12.1* for a summary.)

The first feature focuses on individual faculty, who initially

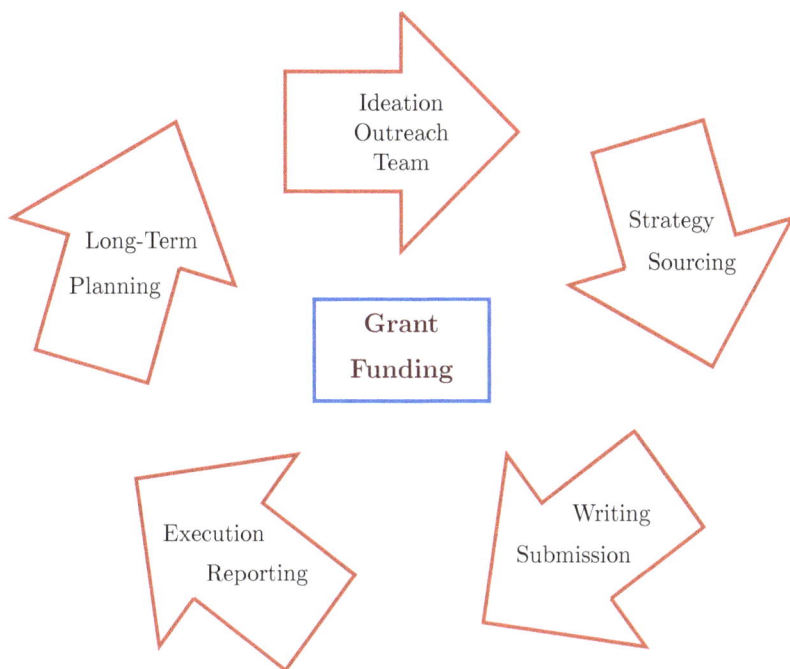

Figure 12.1: The grant flywheel

learn to write grants for their own teaching or scholarship. This often begins with a single small budget proposal, which stimulates thinking ahead to the next grant. For faculty who want to move beyond their own grant activities, this positions them to be a resource for others. Individual grant success can create opportunities to support a growing network of faculty who share an interest in pursuing grants.

Community is what builds a grant culture, so the next step is to encourage colleagues to ask ideation questions regularly. (See *Chapter 3* for details on ideation.) Mentoring is key. It models a grant "attitude" by noticing that there are promising grant prospects all around. Ideas for grants can be sparked by experience, reading, observing, conversation, community outreach, or action.

Individual success draws attention; others will want to emulate it. Indeed, sharing your experiences (in ideation, writing, solicitation searches, and serving on review panels, etc.) helps form a community that increases knowledge, resilience, resources, opportunities, and contacts, which can only improve chances of future success. Fostering discussions (perhaps informally over lunch) to find common interests, exploring interdisciplinary grant prospects, encouraging others to see opportunities in their own ideas, and sharing new resources and knowledge about proposal development help the community blossom.

Building a Bridge

Some suggestions for faculty interested in expanding campus grant activities include:

- Build relationships with trustworthy colleagues willing to discuss ideas, participate in project development, and serve as advisors.

- Extend an awarded grant into other fields by looking through a different lens. Your relationships will create opportunities either for grant renewal/extension or new proposals.

- Think about how to break down big projects in order to prioritize the most fundable elements.

- Look at an idea through an interdisciplinary lens; it will help build relationships and provide additional opportunities.

12.2 Faculty Team Support

In the first feature of a grant culture, activity is initiated and facilitated by the individual writing and submitting a proposal. The driving force in the next feature is the faculty team. In conjunction with individual submissions, several faculty members can come together to identify areas of institutional support that will facilitate future proposal development. These conversations generate the beginnings of an institutional scaffolding that will assist all faculty in pursuing grants.

Scaffolding is a grassroots process that consists of four elements initiated at the faculty level: 1) Share knowledge, 2) Establish institutional guidelines and procedures for proposal development, 3) Create an ad hoc committee(s) to discuss all aspects of proposal development (generate ideas, discuss grant viability, connect colleagues, offer general help, etc.), and 4) Identify a network of college services available.

Through these conversations, faculty will come to realize that the pursuit of grants is more than proposal construction. Grant administration often involves a network of campus services: Human Resources, Accounts Payable, Campus Security, Housing, Food Services, to name a few. The goals of the grant will determine which campus offices to engage. It is essential to build positive relationships with the staff in these offices. First, they possess valuable information on the logistics of campus operations. While faculty are the academic engine of a college, staff are the bureaucratic one, and they also have full schedules to navigate. Second, it helps to brief staff on grant administration procedures so they are prepared ahead of any deadlines. Simply put, relationship building is fundamental to successful grantsmanship and is a step toward an effective grant culture on campus.

12.3   Institutional Grant Culture

The first two features emphasize the fact that any grant pursuit begins at the faculty level. The network initiated by those individual faculty joining together can create an ongoing faculty grant support structure that has a good relationship with campus offices. However, to create a sustainable grant culture embedded in institutional memory, the nexus must be the academic administration. President, provost, and dean are central to weaving this faculty endeavor into the fabric of the institution.

Provosts and deans can facilitate faculty pursuit of grants in two primary ways. One is by earmarking resources in support of proposal development and the other is by officially recognizing faculty efforts: convert ad hoc committees into standing committees (or create standing committees); offer faculty release time, summer stipends, or development funds; create avenues for faculty to share proposal ideas; and incorporate proposal development into the promotion and tenure process. Another important way in which provosts and deans can support faculty is by contacting their counterparts at other institutions in order to initiate opportunities for partnerships.

Finally, provosts and deans, as advocates for their faculty, can communicate to the president the ways in which grant pursuit is an integral part of robust institutional advancement: a grant's indirect costs can contribute to administrative budgets; the development office can use success stories to interest donors; and a history of grant success can lead to an institutional bid for larger strategic grants.

PRACTICE THIS: Finding Prospects

Over the course of a week, create several potential ideas based on your day to day experiences using the examples given here. Build noticing grant prospects into your day, whether from experience, reading, observing, conversation, community outreach, or action. Develop the habit to ask, "How can I turn this into a proposal?" Combine what you find with new context to create original proposals. Always ask, "What's next?" For example, Professor Quinn, after one environmental project came to a close, began looking for other ways to collaborate again with the same community partners. She noticed student interest in a class demo that tested home water for contaminants, and evaluated filters to determine the best way to purify it. Inspired, she developed a concept paper for a portable equipment grant that would extend that simple demo into an environmental project evaluating water quality in regional waterways and investigating income/race-related intersections with water purity.

Chapter 13

Small Business Grants

From Academia to Business

Some academic research and development (R&D) projects can be commercialized.

- The Small Business Innovation Research (SBIR) program assists eligible R&D projects. Projects must match R&D needs of one or more agencies.
- The Small Business Technology Transfer (STTR) program facilitates public/private collaboration. STTR requires a business to have a nonprofit research partner.
- The Silicon Valley Innovation Program (SVIP) supports innovation inside and outside the US to accelerate the transition to market of technology with government applications.

Chapter 13 Glossary

- **Non-dilutive funding:** Financing that does not require the recipient to give up equity in their company.[1] The SVIP program is non-dilutive.

- **Broad Agency Announcement (BAA):** Bulletins used by government agencies to solicit proposals for applied research and development to advance or evaluate cutting-edge technologies.

- **Long Range Broad Agency Announcement (LR-BAA):** Similar to a BAA—the difference is a BAA is relatively specific in its subject matter requirements, a LRBAA is not.

- **Product Pitch:** A three-page white paper that allows start ups and small businesses to get quick feedback at the beginning of their application for Phase I funding from America's SEED Fund powered by the NSF.

- **Cost Match:** A program that can arrange for matching funds from the private sector. This is only offered by the DHS.

- **Opportunity Zones:** An economic development tool that encourages investment in distressed areas in order to spur economic growth and job creation in low-income communities by providing tax benefits to investors.

---

[1]Many of the explanations for the glossary terms are taken from the Department of Homeland Security science and technology website: dhs.gov/science-and-technology/svip

- **SBIR and STTR:** Small Business Innovation Research and Small Business Technology Transfer programs encourage domestic small businesses to engage in federal research and development with the potential for commercialization.

13.1 SBIR/STTR Programs

Federal funding through SBIR/STTR programs support scientific research and technological innovation for critical national priorities. These programs center their missions on promotion and empowerment of businesses with fewer than 500 employees—over half of SBIR/STTR-supported companies have fewer than 25 people—encouraging them to take part in the national research infrastructure, commercialize the results, and contribute to the economy.

Eligible businesses must be US-owned and operated, for-profit entities, and work must happen within the United States and its territories. Because this federal funding is highly competitive, grant priorities must clearly align with a solicitation from one of the eleven participating federal agencies.

Long Range Broad Agency Announcements (LRBAA) and Broad Agency Announcements (BAA) are designed to seek proposals that address broad research areas linked to a funding agency's mission and strategic goals. These announcements may extend for years, are reoccurring, and can become an element in a small business strategic plan.

In addition to fostering participation by small businesses

across the United States and its territories, the SBIR/STTR programs support a diverse portfolio of startups, and target specific groups for inclusion and outreach. These groups include businesses owned by women, people of color, those with disabilities, and entrepreneurs located in socially or economically disadvantaged regions, underserved states, and opportunity zones. The purpose is to spur economic growth and job creation, promote technological creativity, and provide tax benefits to investors.

Tables 13.1 and *13.2* provide a list of federal agencies that fund SBIR/STTR grants. For example, the Department of Transportation offers various high-tech SBIR projects related to railway safety (automation, inspection, assessment, etc.)

Table 13.1: SBIR participating agencies under the supervision of the SBA.

Department of Agriculture	Department of Health and Human Services	Department of Commerce
Department of Homeland Security	Department of Defense	Department of Transportation
Department of Energy	Department of Protection Agency	Department of Education
Department of Foundation	National Aeronautics and Space Administration	

Table 13.2: STTR participating agencies under the supervision of the SBA.

National Science Foundation	National Institute of Standards and Technology	Department of Agriculture
Department of Education	National Oceanic and Atmospheric Administration of the Department of Commerce	

Table 13.3: Summary of SBIR/STTR similarities and differences

Description	SBIR	STTR
Only for-profit businesses with fewer than 500 employees.	✓	✓
Can include an angel investor or venture capitalist as long as majority control is retained by the business.	✓	
Must include a non-profit research institution.		✓
Can include joint ventures as long as the partner firm meets the eligibility requirements.	✓	
Prohibits venture capital investors.		✓
PI must be employed with a small business at least 50% of the time.	✓	
Cannot be used for equipment or technology already fundable through capital markets if those items are already proven or low financial risk.	✓	✓
Funds of $3.2 billion allocated per year.	✓	
Funds of $450 million allocated per year.		✓

13.1.1   SBIR/STTR Program Phases

The SBIR/STTR award structure breaks into three distinct phases.

- **Phase I—Proof of Concept.** The objective of this phase is to demonstrate the merit, feasibility, and commercial potential of the proposed research, as well as to establish the capacity of the small business awardee to implement the entire project. The duration is typically six to twelve months with awards ranging from $50,000 to $275,000

- **Phase II—Technology Development.** Funding is based on Phase I results with a more exhaustive assessment of the scientific/technical merit and the commercial potential of the project. The duration of Phase II is typically 24 months with awards ranging from $750,000 to $1.8 million.

- **Phase III—Commercialization.** There is no funding for this phase. Awardees take their product to the commercial market or sell it in the federal contracting marketplace.

Note: the available SBIR/STTR funding in Fiscal Year 2019 was $54.6 billion[2]

13.1.2   SBIR/STTR Online Resources

The requirements for SBIR/STTR grants vary according to the funding agency, and each solicitation details specific pro-

---

[2]sbir.gov/funding

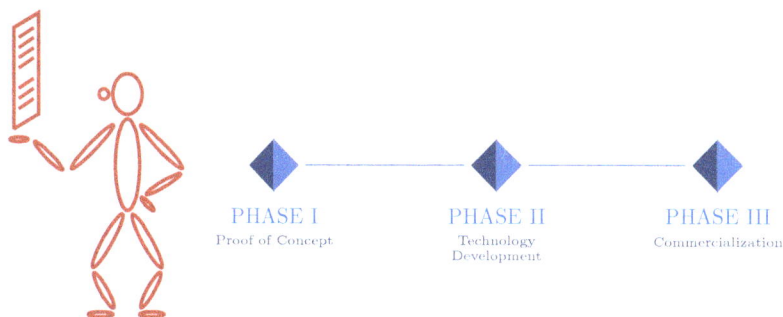

Figure 13.1: SBIR/STTR program phases

posal preparation, submission, and evaluation rules. Most of the agencies also provide application help, resources, and services.[3]. There are several pages at the SBIR website with information about the SBIR/STTR programs, which include a list of current solicitations, templates, and tutorials on how to organize and compose proposals. (See *Table 13.4* for a list of online resources.)

Table 13.4: SBIR/STTR online resources

Home page	sbir.gov/
Comprehensive Tutorials	sbir.gov/tutorials/
Open Agency Solicitations	sbir.gov/solicitations/

13.1.3 The NSF SBIR Project Pitch

The National Science Foundation (NSF) is one of several federal agencies that requires SBIR applicants to first sub-

---

[3]A list of local organizations that can assist SBIR/STTR applicants can be found at sbir.gov/local-assistance/

mit a three-page project pitch to the NSF America's Seed Fund program. This project pitch must be approved in order to apply for Phase I. It is a brief sketch of the proposed project—no more than 1500 words. The brevity allows review panels to work quickly, which enables applicants to get swift and responsive feedback, usually in three weeks. NSF staff are available to provide some guidance whether or not the pitch is accepted, which will help you determine whether re-submission is possible. If the project pitch fits the goals of America's Seed Fund, an official invitation will be issued by the NSF to submit a full proposal.

The project pitch contains four elements.

- **Technology Innovation (500 words).** This element discusses how a project meets the NSF mandate to support R&D of new, high-impact innovations in technology. Include a description of how the idea qualifies as being an innovative product, process, or service.

- **Technical Objectives/Challenges (500 words).** This portion demonstrates technically feasibility, impact on current state-of-the-art technology, and commercial viability. The project must represent more than incremental engineering or product improvement.

- **Market Opportunity(250 words).** This section describes the market and consumer base for the product. Include both potential problems and solutions in its commercialization.

- **Company and Team Qualifications (250 words).** This part discusses the current status of the small business. Moreover, it documents team expertise and experience, and demonstrates their capacity to contribute to project success.

More information can be found at seedfund.nsf.gov/project-pitch/.

13.1.4 DHS SBIR Cost Match

Another federal agency that requires a project pitch is the DHS Science and Technology division. Additionally, this Division has a cost match requirement for Phase II of SBIR, in which the DHS can arrange to match 50% of private sector investment of at least $100,000 (for a maximum DHS match of $250,000).

More information can be found at sbir2.st.dhs.gov.

13.2 SVIP

Start-ups can be laboratories for innovation. The Silicon Valley Innovation Program (SVIP) supports the development of prototypes that can strengthen homeland and national security, particularly in the areas of cybersecurity, customs and border protection, and first responder operations. SVIP facilitates innovative technology transitioning to market, strengthening the working partnership between entrepreneurs and the government. SVIP targets and engages start-up enterprises with up to $2 million in non-dilutive funding over 24 months.

Table 13.5: Benefits of the SVIP program

There are numerous benefits to the SVIP program
Targets startup businesses.
Grants awards within 45 days of proposal submission.
Provides funding for upfront costs, including equipment upgrades.
Enables applicant to retain intellectual property rights while giving the government a license agreement.
Offers potential followup for promising technologies and sponsorship for user test case prototypes.
Positions the applicant for future funding with DHS and other agencies.

SVIP uses a streamlined pitch process like the SBIR. In addition to this pitch process, SVIP a has four-phase (instead of three) award structure.

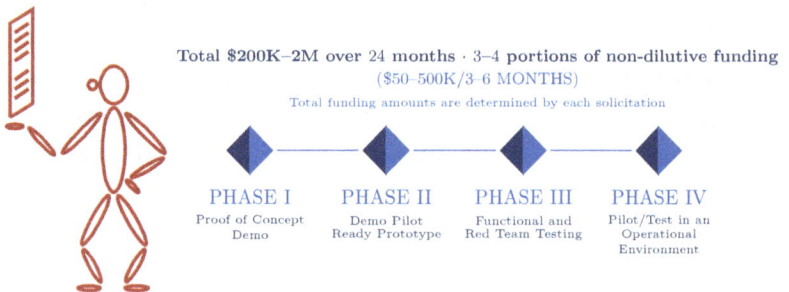

Total $200K–2M over 24 months · 3–4 portions of non-dilutive funding ($50–500K/3–6 MONTHS)

Total funding amounts are determined by each solicitation

PHASE I — Proof of Concept Demo

PHASE II — Demo Pilot Ready Prototype

PHASE III — Functional and Red Team Testing

PHASE IV — Pilot/Test in an Operational Environment

Figure 13.2: SVIP phases

An SVIP Phase V may be awarded if the government determines that further operational testing is required, and/or the technology is applicable in additional DHS use cases. Phase V Other Transactional Agreements will be scaled to fit the cost and length of time for the mission need/requirement and are not restricted by Phases I – IV.

13.3 The Future

By championing the search to find new technologies, the SBIR, STTR, and the SVIP strengthen national security while they work towards the goal of reshaping how government, entrepreneurs, and industry work together to find cutting-edge solutions. These three programs enable government to support small business in finding new technology and addressing urgent technological issues.

PRACTICE THIS: Searching for Opportunities

Pursuit of SBIR/STTR grants is good motivation for undergraduates who are often enthusiastic to extend their academic projects beyond the classroom.

Accelerant Detection Canines (ADC) are dogs trained to uncover a variety of ignitable liquids that could be used to initiate a fire. ADCs are currently more accurate than mechanical sniffer devices; however, there are numerous disadvantages.[a] Two biology majors are creating the next generation of sniffer algorithms that will make it possible for drones to better detect ignitable liquids.

Go to sbir.gov/sbirsearch/topic/current

- Scan a list of current and upcoming topic areas and identify some that align with developing sniffer algorithms for drones.

- Scan the history of past SBIR/STTR solicitations across all participating agencies to determine similar projects that were previously funded.

---

[a]Technology Against Terrorism: Structuring Security. (1994). (n.p.): DIANE Publishing Company.

Appendix A

Ideation Examples

Inspiration for proposal ideas is everywhere. Examples have been used throughout the book to emphasize a point or to demonstrate a feature of proposal development. In this appendix we present some examples in the hopes it will fire the imagination. These topics could be applied toward a research project, development of educational materials, or student-oriented projects.

A.1 Sustainability

Sustainability is a rich arena for proposal ideas, whether focused on research, education, or workforce development. Topics range from climate change to management of natural resources, sustainable human environments, responding to natural disasters, data-aware energy use, and global change. For example, sustainability topics are good for a summer workshop that targets first-generation students from under-represented groups.

A.1.1   Climate-friendly technologies

New technologies are often introduced with the pitch that they will reduce the types of pollution that exacerbate global change. However, a new technology that addresses a current issue often creates new, and/or worsens other problems. For example, electric vehicles (EV) continue to increase their footprint within the auto industry. While EVs have a smaller imprint on carbon emissions, they are not pollution-free and they impact the economy of precious metals and minerals (lithium, cobalt, nickel, graphite, manganese, copper, etc.). How will this affect global economics and politics? What other new sustainable technologies might enter the market and result in less pollution?

A.1.2   Invasive Species

Invasive species are pervade most ecosystems. Since the Colombian exchange, modern commerce and travel have completely transformed continental environments. Some invasive species contribute to the economy and have been completely integrated into the ecosystem (honeybees, farm stock, fruit trees and vines, etc.). Others cause more damage than good. A project investigating invasive species could be one that focuses on research or education.

A.1.3   Local versus global

News on global change often concentrates on global impact. This can be discouraging if someone wants to focus on improving their neighborhood because micro-environments may differ from the global one. Studies that examine how environmental efforts can impact local change could find a friendly audience with regional private foundations. For example, a program could promote a student project that develops a lawn conversion plan for school property.

A.1.4   Data-aware energy use

A significant quantity of research exists on creating self-managing energy systems for buildings that operate with only "high level" guidance from humans.[1] There is still room for more research, such as model-driven energy management for smart buildings and development of tools for energy-efficient buildings. There are also opportunities for connecting this research to all levels of education. For example, grants are available for the creation of educational tools that demonstrate the importance of sustainable energy usage. Moreover, grants are available for educational activities focused on network optimization and traffic modeling, among other ideas.

A.2   Community-Oriented Ideas

Community-oriented projects benefit both the surrounding region and the institution. Most institutions have a Com-

---

[1] archive.dimacs.rutgers.edu/Workshops/EnergyUse/abstracts.html

munity Engagement Office with resources and contacts that faculty can use to get started thinking about grant potential.

A.2.1   Community Improvement

Community improvement grants are available through government agencies and private foundations. These are usually small, but can have a large impact.[2] Colleges and universities could partner with the local municipality to apply for such grants.[3] Some suggestions include:

- Restore historical sites such as a local cemetery, old water pump station, one-room schoolhouse, colonial-era structure, mill, or many other projects.

- Convert an empty or abandoned lot into a public space or garden.

- Develop a restoration project for an ecosystem, such as daylighting a stream or reforesting a field.

A.2.2   Community History

America is a nation of immigrants. As the first generation ages, it would be good to capture this group's impact on American cultural change including music, visual and performing arts, agriculture, foodways, technology, architecture, and many more. One suggestion would be to

---

[2]Community projects are a good way to facilitate better relations between an institution and its external community.

[3]kab.org/beautification/community-grants/
dced.pa.gov/housing-and-development/community-development-block-grant/
hud.gov/program_offices/comm_planning/cdbg

record their memories and experiences within the community. Small grants are often available to support these kinds of projects.

A.2.3   Community Organizations

Partnering with community organizations is a rewarding experience. Community engagement offices have established connections with regional family service organizations (FSO), churches, nature conservancies, and other public service establishments. FSOs in particular are always searching for ways to extend and expand their programs. Small grants exist to support summer camps, after-school educational workshops, and family programs. A summer camp can be an excellent device to encourage students to be the first in their family to attend college. Program funds should include breakfast, lunch, and transportation to and from the institution. Consider:

- A program that develops arts and crafts skills that include information on careers and entrepreneurial opportunities.

- An examination of the health and stability of local ecosystems in order to identify native and invasive species, as well as conserve and preserve the environment.

- Imaginative applications of science and mathematics can encourage interest in scientific careers.

A.3   Arts and Humanities

In *Chapter 3* we explore some of the majors resources available for projects in the Arts and Humanities: National Endowment for the Arts, National Endowment for the Humanities, city grants, Library of Congress, Some ideation suggestions include the following.

A.3.1   Travel Funds

One common solicitation in all fields is for travel supporting research and professional development. For instance,

- Travel to the Library of Congress to research The Poet Laureates of the last 30 years to study the face of poetry in the US today.

- Travel to interview members of a performance organization such as the Alvin Ailey Dance Company to investigate the influence of professional African-American companies on American dance.

- Funding undergraduate travel as part of course content: studying the city in literature by traveling to three capital cities.

A.3.2   Production Projects

Another common solicitation area supports specific production projects across disciplines. For example, funding public art, video production, collaborative community arts projects, retrospectives, or celebrating underrepresented cultures or histories.

A.3.3 Organizational Renewal

There are solicitations that support such projects as historical renovations of buildings, enhancing collections, and sourcing content for exhibitions.

Appendix B

Internal Checklist

Before you submit (or even write) a proposal, make certain that you have discussed and coordinated logistics for your potential project with all of the relevant administrative offices and committees at your institution. Many of these items will not apply to your project, but some always do; contact grants and development personnel as soon as possible in advance, and maintain continuous coordination with them. They can guide you as you work through the checklist below. We tried to categorize questions into departments, but your institution may do things differently. You may need to add items to this list, or you may not know which committee handles some questions. Talk to your department chair, then a dean, and finally a provost for answers.

Grants Office or Committee

☐ What organizational rules apply to faculty grant writing?

  ☐ Is release time an option to help manage the grant?

  ☐ Will grant-writing be considered in promotion and tenure review?

☐ What administrative offices need to be consulted?

☐ What departments or committees deal with various aspects of grant administration? Who are the best contacts in those groups?

  ☐ Expenses

  ☐ Payroll

  ☐ Human Resources

  ☐ Institutional Review Board (IRB)

  ☐ Equipment and Technology

  ☐ Venues: Event Spaces and Services

  ☐ Food Service

  ☐ Shuttle Service

☐ What staff are available to support events?

☐ Are external partnerships permitted, and if so, what are the requirements? Guidelines?

☐ Who on campus might serve as mentor to this grant effort?

☐ Are there other offices or support people on your campus?

Staff

☐ Arrange staff assistance with administrators. Faculty may initiate communications with staff, but administrators will make assignments and organize or facilitate these meetings. Institutional realities mean personnel resources may be stretched or unavailable.

☐ Get staff input on how best to proceed with their offices. If a necessary process does not exist for an office, help develop one.

☐ How much advance notice will staff need to respond to requests?

☐ What online or hardcopy forms need to be filled out?

☐ Create needed templates for proposal components with staff input.

☐ Will staff need funding for summer hours? How should you arrange this?

Research Team

☐ What experience is needed on the team?

☐ Who will coordinate what?

☐ Are there a sufficient number of experts at your institution? If not, are you able to coordinate with knowledgeable people from a potential partner?

Facilities and Services

☐ What space is required? When? Is the space shared with other programs?

☐ What equipment is needed? Will instructions be given to participants?

☐ Will participants be given access to WiFi? Will temporary accounts be assigned or is guest access sufficient?

☐ Will off-campus venues need to be reserved?

☐ How will the program pay for meals (debit versus catered)?

    ☐ What kinds of catering can be provided, e.g. special dietary requirements for participants?

    ☐ Where are dining location(s) on and off campus?

    ☐ What is the procedure for reserving a dining location?

☐ What is the procedure for reserving space and equipment?

☐ What department space is available?

☐ How will you assess available facilities for program needs, e.g. technology, size, etc.?

- [ ] What equipment should be in meeting rooms?

Housing

- [ ] Will participants require on-campus or off-campus housing?
- [ ] Are competing bids required for off-campus housing?
- [ ] What are the procedures and regulations for securing off-campus housing?
- [ ] If on-campus, will linens and cleaning be provided to participants?
- [ ] How will participants be shuttled to and from campus?

Human Resources

- [ ] Are there required forms?
    - [ ] Photo release?
    - [ ] Background checks?
    - [ ] Parental approval for participating minors?
- [ ] Is legal approval required for changes to HR documents or other communication?
- [ ] What accommodations are needed for any participating minors?
- [ ] Are childcare accommodations needed?
- [ ] Do participants receive a stipend, and how will it be distributed?

☐ Will there be visa issues for foreign participants enrolled in the program? (See also Accounts Payable)

☐ Are there restrictions on paying foreign participants, even if they have current visas? Some federal grants have this restriction and some do not. (See also Accounts Payable)

IRB/IACUC

☐ What IRB or Institutional Animal Care and Use Committee (IACUC) approval level is required?

☐ What is the process for getting approval?

Accounts Payable

☐ What constitutes indirect costs at your institution and how are they handled?

☐ What is your institution's Negotiated Indirect Costs Rate Agreement (NICRA)? (See *Section 7.3.3.*)

☐ How are taxes handled for stipends versus work study versus honoraria?

☐ How will you store records and receipts of expenditures in the institution's system?

☐ Is timely submission of reports tied to the release of the next round of funds?

☐ What is the preferred payment method: reimbursement versus direct payment?

☐ What is the best way to pay stipends and honoraria so grant funding criteria are met? (Institutions have different processes and some may be unaware of all the IRS rules and caveats.)

☐ Will there be visa issues for foreign participants enrolled in the program? (See also Human Resources)

☐ Are there restrictions on paying foreign participants, even if they have current visas? Some federal grants have this restriction and some do not. (See also Human Resources)

Evaluation

☐ Is the Institutional Research office eligible to serve as the grant project evaluator?

☐ What data does this office need in order to evaluate your grant?

☐ If the office does not plan to serve as the evaluator, will they find or at least recommend an outside evaluator for your grant project?

☐ Does the office have a template for a data management plan that you could adapt for your grant project? (Federal grants, for example, require public dissemination, so it is important to have a dissemination plan.)

Campus Security

☐ How will participants arrive on campus?

☐ What are the rules for parking?

☐ How will participants navigate campus?

☐ Do participants need a campus ID? Where and when will it be available?

Appendix C

Professional Editing

- **Write and edit separately.** Writing—ideas, evidence, outlines, raw paragraphs—is a fundamentally different activity from editing those components into a coherent, reasoned, grammatically correct whole. Trying to write and edit at the same time often slows things down.
- **Ask at least one other person to proofread and critique.** No one can self-edit completely. There will always be faulty logic or typos that the original writer cannot see.

C.1   Editing Levels

Editors and publishing houses categorize editing levels in different ways, which often overlap and include re-writing; however, there are three major divisions.

Developmental editing considers the big picture—the whole document—and suggests improvements in coherence, organization, focus, and argumentation.

Substantive editing is narrower in scope, focuses on the writing and how the document flows from one paragraph to another. It may include rearranging sentences, choosing more appropriate vocabulary, evaluating the logic and weight of evidence, and so on.

Copy editing focuses on the individual sentence and corrects typographical errors, subject-verb agreement, voice, tone, and so on. It is mostly about correct English usage for a particular audience.

C.2   Recommended Editing Books

Some are out of print, although still useful and available secondhand. Most have multiple editions, with only one cited here. The first two are immediately useful for editing. The third is a widely-used college-level textbook on analytical writing. The fourth is a classic on displaying large data sets with clear, accurate graphics. The final two are textbooks for professional editors.

- **Revising Prose, by Richard Lanham, Pearson Publishing, 2006, ISBN #978-0321441690**

If you only have time for one book on editing, this is it. Lanham devised the "Paramedic Method" of keeping the writing alive until you can save it, by using active voice, strong verbs, rhythm, emphasis, no clutter, and minimized prepositions. You will need other editing techniques as well, but this set provides a big head start.

- **The Elephants of Style, Bill Walsh, McGraw Hill 2004, ISBN #978-0071422680**

Walsh, as the title shows, riffs on (and debunks some of) Strunk and White. One chapter relates, "Lies your English Teacher Told You." Another reports, "Great Moments in Obfuscation." Walsh deals mostly with usage rather than general revision, but both the Lanham and Walsh books work well together.

- **Writing Analytically, Jill Stephen and David Rosenwasser, Cengage Learning, 9th ed., 2023, ISBN #978-0357793657**

The ninth edition of this classic adds more material on how to think about and structure analytical writing. It is a comprehensive textbook.

- **The Visual Display of Quantitative Information, Edward Tufte, Graphics Press, 2001, ISBN #978-0961392147**

Tufte, a statistician who specializes in informational graphics, wrote this elaborately illustrated volume to examine and critique representations of large data sets. He refers to bad data graphics (regrettably common) as "chartjunk." Consult this book if you need complex diagrams or graphs in your proposal to convey a difficult concept pictorially. Please note: some granting agencies do not allow visual entries, so check the solicitation.

- **The Subversive Copy Editor, Carol Fisher Saller, U. Chicago Press, 2016, ISBN #978-0-226-24007-7.**

Saller writes not so much about the nuts and bolts of copyediting (any style manual will provide the rules of grammar and usage), but instead about strengthening the professional relationship between editor and writer in order to improve outcomes, important for any team effort at writing a complex document like a grant proposal.

- **Developmental Editing: A Handbook for Freelancers, Authors, and Publishers, Scott Norton, U. Chicago Press, 2009, ISBN #978-0-226-59515-3.**

Norton's book is a dense textbook on developmental editing, with in-depth examples from multiple fields. Chapters include concept, content, thesis, narrative, exposition, plan, rhythm, transitions, style, and display.

C.3 Editing Example 1

John F. Kennedy wrote his Harvard senior thesis on the run-up to WWII, entitled: "Appeasement at Munich: The Inevitable Result of the Slowness of Conversion of the British Democracy from a Disarmament to a Rearmament Policy."

The published book's eventual title? "Why England Slept."

As academics, we navigate lots of prose like the original title, and sometimes admittedly write it, but it is needlessly difficult. Kennedy eventually published a best-selling book based on his thesis. It must have been a fairly extreme editing job; notice how much shorter the final title is. It is much more intriguing, too. As a metaphor, it suggests lots of subtext, and it riffs off Churchill's earlier book title "While England Slept."

C.3.1 Metaphors and Tone

Metaphors can be useful in a proposal. If, for example, your education grant submission begins with a few dense data paragraphs on the enormous obstacles first-generation undergraduates face trying to navigate college culture, try ending that with a sentence that expresses the problem visually. "These students essentially drop into another country with few language skills, no landscape maps, and little guidance on how to get started."

This would be appropriate for a particular kind of solicitation, perhaps one that was targeting the specific problems of these students. It communicates urgency and a relatable context in a somewhat activist tone. But be careful about tone and audience. Would such a metaphor appear in an NSF proposal on a new molecule? Probably not. The take-away here: match your tone and language to the proposal's audience.

C.4　Quick Editing Hits

Four main techniques from the books recommended here will help clarify language and sentence structure that either obstructs or fails to add meaning. Additionally, because grant solicitations often limit the number of pages, these techniques will usually shorten a manuscript that exceeds page limitations.

- Reconfigure most prepositional phrases. Long strings of them are particularly hard on the reader (notice the word "of" repeated in the example in *Section C.3*).

- Remove weak verbs and avoid the passive voice, both of which dilute writing and reduce the impact of any sentence. Instead, install precise active verbs near the subject. You can find good candidates in many parts of speech. (See *Section C.5* for a paragraph with potential active verbs italicized.)

- Clear out needless blather. Delete any hemming and hawing before, during, or after the sentence. Make your proposal's case directly and without chatter.

- Develop a good "ear" for the English language—sound, word choice, sentence length, rhythm. Read it aloud, preferably to another person. Notice how simply varying sentence length can improve matters; paragraphs in which the sentences are all the same length tend to be boring to read, no matter how much useful information they contain.

Notice that you need not get rid of all the prepositions, passive voice, and weak verbs, but use them strategically, only when necessary for your particular proposal and audience.

C.5 Editing Example 2

A conference presentation abstract appears in *Section C.5.1*, unchanged from the original except for the markups: **boldfaced** prepositions, underlined weak verbs and passive voice, *italicized* active verb candidates, and ~~strike-through~~ grammar errors. Additionally, the sentence lengths are marked off with //.

This abstract communicates important, complete information and does not exceed the conference word limit, but a colleague asked if we could streamline it and make it more engaging. She studies small molecules that can cross the blood-brain barrier, a serious need in the pharmaceutical industry and thus ripe for a grant (although a grant is not the subject of this paragraph, it could stimulate one). We also shortened the passage without losing any meaning, which makes it more likely that busy conference-goers will read it.

C.5.1   Original Paragraph

Despite the significant impact that drugs have had **on** our society, the process **by** which a drug is *discovered* and *developed* is poorly *understood* **by** the general public.// This limited understanding has, **in** part, *triggered* widespread conspiracy theories and public criticisms, especially pertaining **to** the cost **of** drugs.// Courses **about** drug discovery and the pharmaceutical industry could *benefit* all students; however, many courses *developed* **to** date are *intended* **for** science majors.// **At** XYZ College, we *developed* a cross-disciplinary non-majors course **about** the pharmaceutical industry titled "Pharma: Friend or Foe?" This course, called a cluster course, was *offered* **for** the first time **in** the spring **of** 2017, and it *contributes* towards the college's integrative learning requirement.// This cluster ~~is comprised of~~ two courses **from** separate disciplines: one **on** the scientific perspective **of** the industry, taught **by** Professor SY, and the other **on** an ethical perspective **of** the industry, taught **by** Professor GC.// **In** the scientific course, students are *introduced* **to** molecular structure, pharmacokinetics, small molecule and biologic drugs, and the FDA, **as well as** marketing and manufacturing **in** the industry.// Students also *explore* why drugs are so costly and why they take so long to *develop*.// **In** the ethics course, students *debate* the role **of** lobbyists and politics **in** the industry and the ethical issues *surrounding* animal testing. A course overview and schedule, sample assignments, preliminary assessment data, and reflections **by** the instructors will be *presented*.//

C.5.2 Original Paragraph Analysis

The original paragraph presents an innovative teaching concept with essential background and societal relevance. It already employs some good active verbs, only makes one serious grammar error, avoids chaining prepositional phrases together (although there are quite a few), and varies sentence length pretty well. An edit should preserve the meaning of the passage while at the same time:

- Clarify the two different courses and who teaches what;

- Reduce needless repetition and overused words;

- Add more active voice;

- Avoid unfortunate subtexts;

- Reduce some of the prepositional phrases;

- Change or remove the one grammar error;

- Add more examples and data where possible.

C.5.3 Edited Paragraph

Despite the significant positive impact that medicines have had **on** our society, the public little *understands* the process **of** drug discovery and development, which tends to *trigger* health conspiracy theories and other criticisms, especially pertaining **to** cost, risk, efficacy, and side effects.// College courses **in** this field often *target* science majors, but **at** XYZ College, we *created* (Spring 2017) a cross-disciplinary non-majors course **about** the pharmaceutical industry titled "Pharma: Friend or Foe?"// Structured **as** a "cluster"—two different courses *linking* common themes and assignments—it *fulfills* part **of** the college's integrative learning requirement.// **On** the science side, taught **by** Professor SY, students *learn* molecular structure, pharmacokinetics, small molecule and biologic drugs, plus marketing, time **to** market, pricing, manufacturing, and FDA regulation.// **On** the ethics side, taught **by** Professor GC, students *debate* the role **of** lobbyists and politics **in** the industry, and the ethical issues surrounding animal testing.// The instructors will *present* a course overview and schedule, sample assignments, preliminary assessment data, and their own reflections.

C.5.4 Edited Paragraph Changes

- Without any loss of meaning, sentence combination, preposition reduction (by half), and most (not all) passive voice removal shortened the passage by about 60 words.

- Additional evidence (risk, efficacy, side effects in addition to the original cost), more precise parallel construction (science side / ethics side), and improved word choice ("medicine" rather than "drug," which can suggest illegality) enhanced clarity.

- Finally, word substitution removed some repetition (one instance of "develop" in contrast to four in the original, for example).

C.5.5 Original versus Edited

Table C.1: Side-by-side editing comparison

Original Paragraph	Edited Paragraph
Despite the significant impact that drugs have had **on** our society, the process **by** which a drug is *discovered* and *developed* is poorly *understood* **by** the general public.// This limited understanding has, **in** part, *triggered* widespread conspiracy theories and public criticisms, especially pertaining **to** the cost **of** drugs.// Courses **about** drug discovery and the pharmaceutical industry could *benefit* all students; however, many courses *developed* **to** date are *intended* **for** science majors.// **At** XYZ College, we *developed* a cross-disciplinary non-majors course **about** the pharmaceutical industry titled "Pharma: Friend or Foe?" This course, called a cluster course, was *offered* **for** the first time **in** the spring **of** 2017, and it *contributes* towards the college's integrative learning requirement.// This cluster is comprised of two courses **from** separate disciplines: one **on** the scientific perspective **of** the industry, taught **by** Professor SY, and the other **on** an ethical perspective **of** the industry, taught **by** Professor GC.// **In** the scientific course, students are *introduced* **to** molecular structure, pharmacokinetics, small molecule and biologic drugs, and the FDA, **as well as** marketing and manufacturing **in** the industry.// Students also *explore* why drugs are so costly and why they take so long to *develop*.// In the ethics course, students *debate* the role **of** lobbyists and politics **in** the industry and the ethical issues *surrounding* animal testing. A course overview and schedule, sample assignments, preliminary assessment data, and reflections **by** the instructors will be *presented*.	Despite the significant positive impact that medicines have had **on** our society, the public little *understands* the process **of** drug discovery and development, which tends to *trigger* health conspiracy theories and other criticisms, especially pertaining **to** cost, risk, efficacy, and side effects.// College courses **in** this field often *target* science majors, but **at** XYZ College, we *created* (Spring 2017) a cross-disciplinary non-majors course **about** the pharmaceutical industry titled "Pharma: Friend or Foe?"// Structured **as** a "cluster"—two different courses *linking* common themes and assignments—it *fulfills* part **of** the college's integrative learning requirement.// **On** the science side, taught **by** Professor SY, students *learn* molecular structure, pharmacokinetics, small molecule and biologic drugs, plus marketing, time **to** market, pricing, manufacturing, and FDA regulation.// **On** the ethics side, taught **by** Professor GC, students *debate* the role **of** lobbyists and politics **in** the industry, and the ethical issues surrounding animal testing.// The instructors will *present* a course overview and schedule, sample assignments, preliminary assessment data, and their own reflections.

Index